FROM THE ASHEN LAND OF THE VIRGIN

CONVERSATIONS WITH BIOY CASARES, BORGES, DENEVI, ETCHECOPAR, OCAMPO, OROZCO, SABATO
IN ARGENTINA

RAUL GALVEZ

MOSAIC PRESS
Oakville – New York – London

CANADIAN CATALOGUING IN PUBLICATION DATA

Galvez, Raul, 1946–
    From the ashen land of the virgin

ISBN 0-88962-347-3 (bound)   ISBN 0-88962-346-5 (pbk.)

1. Authors, Argentine – Interviews. 2. Argentine
literature – 20th century – History and criticism.
I. Bioy Casares, Adolfo. II. Title.

PQ7653.G35 1988   860'.9   C88-093623-1

Published by MOSAIC PRESS, P.O. Box 1032, Oakville, Ontario,
L6J 5E9, Canada. Offices and warehouse at 1252 Speers Road,
Units# 1&2, Oakville, Ontario, L6L 5N9, Canada.

Mosaic Press acknowledges the assistance of the Canada Council
and the Ontario Arts Council in support of its publishing pro-
gramme.

Copyright © Raul Galvez, 1989
Design by Rita Vogel
Cover photo by Raul Galvez
Cover Design by Marion Black
Typeset by Bambam Type & Graphics
Printed and bound in Canada.   boo356299 2   C

ISBN 0-88962-346-5 PAPER   ISBN 0-88962-347-3 CLOTH c

MOSAIC PRESS:
In Canada:
        MOSAIC PRESS, 1252 Speers Road, Units# 1&2, Oakville,
Ontario L6J 5N9, Canada. P.O. Box 1032, Oakville, Ontario L6J 5E9

In the United States:
        Riverrun Press Inc., 1170 Broadway, Suite 807, New York,
N.Y., 10001, U.S.A., distributed by Kampmann & Co., 9 East 40th
Street, New York, N.Y., 10016

In the U.K.:
        John Calder (Publishers) Ltd., 18 Brewer Street, London,
W1R 4A5, England.

FROM THE ASHEN LAND OF THE VIRGIN

CONVERSATIONS WITH

ES,
AR,
BATO

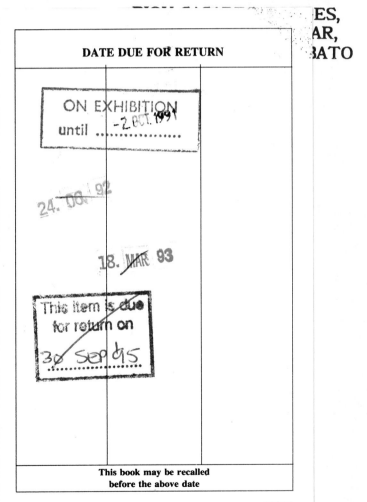

PROLOGUE

Going back to Argintina, my native country, after six years living in Canada, forced me to make a series of comparisons between countries. I left a nation governed by the military - something for which they obviously were noot educated - and came back to a democratic Argentina. If today Argentina is a disorder trying to correct itself, Canada is, comparatively, an excessive order running the risk of self indulgence. If Argentina,as many other countries in Latin America, has produced the quantity of artists it has produced, it is not because chaos is "creative". But precisely as a reaction against that chaos that pervades everything.

But to explain the flourishing of artists and intellectuals only for socio-politico-econimic reasons would be naive and false. The reasons for creation are much deeper and mysterious.

If art is the soul and spirit of a society, we should resort to that well to know it intimately. That was the starting point for these interviews, initially intended for a radio program in Toronto. Hopefully this book will serve as a stimulus to bring readers closer to the works of these authors.

Seeing the poor distribution Argentinian writers and poets have in Canada, propelled this idea into print. I would have liked to include many more, but that is material for another book.

Argentina and Canada belong to the two extremes of America: geographical, political and linguistic. Perhaps through the voice of some Argentinian creators, a bridge may be built to lessen that distance.

R.G.
October 1986.
Toronto.

ACKNOWLEDGMENTS

To Susana Wald, Ludwig Zeller and Kim Obrist, without whose help this book would not have been possible.

These interviews were originally done in Spanish. I have translated into English for this edition with the invaluable assistance of Kim Obrist. She was also in charge of the correction and supervision into that language.

R.G.

FOREWARD

"From the Ashen Land of the Virgin"

After trying different titles for this book without success, a phrase from a poem I wrote after my visit to Buenos Aires came to mind: "...from the Ashen Land of the Virgin". It seemed to synthesize painful but hopeful impressions of Buenos Aires and Argentina. Ashen Land because:

In Argentinian history, so full of terrible, bloody battles and internal and external wars, the fire has not yet been extinguished under the ashes.

The decadence of the ruling class; the moral and political corruption at all social levels; Liberalism (one among many "isms" but perhaps the principal one that has practically reduced the country to ruins) are only part of the visible wreckage of an immobile nation. Argentina then, should re-emerge from the ashes this time peacefully, if she wants to recover the greatness for which she was singularly suited.

"Land of the Virgin" because:
Argentina has always had a strong Marion tradition. Since the founding of Buenos Aires, a city whose original name "Puerto Nuestra Señora Santa Maria del Buen Ayre" (Port of Our Lady Holy Mary of Fair Wind) was given in 1536 by Pedro de Mendoza. It was in hommage to the "Virgen Sarda del Santuario de Cagliari" (Italy) ("The Sardinian Virgin of the Cagliari Sanctuary"), patroness of sailors.

For the innumerable churches built throughout the country under Her protection and name; for General San Martin - the hero and Liberator of South America - who warned his men that "the tongue that dares to blaspheme against Her would be pierced with red iron"; for the famous annual pilgrimages to the Virgin of Lujan (Bs.As.) and to the recent apparitions reported in San Nicolas (Bs.As.), now under study by a Church commission; for these and all the historical facts too numerous to mention here, Argentina is "The Ashen Land of the Virgin".

Raul Galvez
January 1988.
Toronto.

Table of Contents

*B*orn 15 September, 1914, in Buenos Aires, Adolfo Bioy Casares is the son of diplomat Adolfo Bioy, a French descendant from the Bearn region, and Marta Casares. She was a very beautiful and cultured woman, who based her life on the philosophy of the stoics, and in this sense influenced her son. Prominent local artists, writers and personalities visiting Argentina, would gather at their house in Buenos Aires, in an atmosphere of friendship and culture.

At the age of nine, he falls in love with a cousin and writes a novel "Iris y Margarita" copying the type of books she likes. He doesn't get further than the first three chapters. He starts reading "The Book of Animals" by Buffon, "Pinocchio" by Collodi and "The Adventures of Dick Turpin". He starts writing on the most various themes, and by the age of 23, he has written about 12 voluminous pieces of unpublished or unfinished work. He called this period, the learning process.

In 1924 for the first time he travels to Europe with his parents. He is ten years old, and that will be the start of long trips throughout his life.

In 1928 he reads Gaston Leroux and Sherlock Holmes. He writes his first thriller "Vanidad o Una aventura terrorifica". In 1929 under his father's protection and support, he publishes his first book "Prologo". His readings includes The Bible, The Divine Comedy and Ulysses. Writing as a profession doesn't occur to him. He wants to be perhaps, an engineer, a film director or above all world champion of tennis.

In 1931 he is given Ayax, a mottled Great Dane, which is to be his favourite dog. He reads Nietzche, Kant, and at his mother's suggestion "Marcus Aurelius" by Epicteto. His parents' advice was to "read any book as long as it's good".

That same year in Buenos Aires, the first issue of "SUR" appears. It is a prestigious literary magazine collection directed by Victoria Ocampo. She will become one of Argentina's leading cultural luminaries. At her house, he meets Jorge Luis Borges in 1932. Their friendship and collaboration are to last a lifetime.

In 1933 the mass market publishing house TOR accepts "17 Disparos contra lo porvenir", a collection of short stories. He gives up his law studies and begins at the University of Philosophy & Literature, but feels even further removed from literature. "In an exam" he says "I compared - God forgive me - Baudelaire, Rimbaud, Verlaine and Mallarme's poems to sentimental tango lyrics. Perhaps out of pity, the professors passed me". He reads the Russians, Berkeley and Hume.

In 1934 he meets Silvina Ocampo. The book of short stories "Caos" is published and badly received by the critics. Borges and Silvina Ocampo advise him to abandon University and write full time. He discovers Wells, Conrad, Chesterton, Shaw, Kipling.

The following year he convinces his father to let him run the family "estancia" in Pardo, in the province of Buenos Aires. He becomes fully immersed in it.His first novel "La nueva tormenta" is published with Silvina Ocampo's drawings. He reads books about relativity and the fourth dimension.

In 1936, Borges and he founded the magazine "Destiempo". It lasts only three issues. The short stories of "La estatua casera" are published and the following year "Luis Greve, muerto".

In 1940 he marries Silvina Ocampo. A poet, painter and a writer herself, sister of Victoria, she will become one of Argentina's finest artists. That same year he publishes "The invention of Morel": a landmark in his career. After their marriage, to really discover Argentina, he and Silvina bought a motor home. It was called "the puigper" and Ayax will go with them. Due to the dangers and complications of the journey, they sell the vehicle in the province of Cordoba, and return to Buenos Aires. The trio then (Bioy Casares, Borges, Silvina Ocampo) compile the "Antologia de la Literatura Fantastica".

He reads voraciously: Schopenhauer, Murasaki, Lei Shonogon, Alexandra Davis' books about Tibet, Neel books about symbolic logic and Galton's "Inquiries into Human Faculties".

In 1941, at the age of 27, he receives the First Buenos Aires Municipal Prize of Literature for "The invention of Morel". He publishes "Antologia Poetica Argentina" with Borges and Silvina Ocampo.

In 1942, Borges and he created the character Isidro Parodi, a detective who solves cases from his prison cell. The book is called "Six problems for Don Isidro Parodi" under the pseudonym H. Bustos Domecq. His dog Ayax dies. Silvina Ocampo depicted Ayax in her book "Los dias de la noche". She says he was "tiger-like, with cold, little ears. His eyes were the colour of yellow pond waters, and when he got angry, they turned grey. Standing on his back feet, he was as big as a man. I was touched, as he was so big yet had such cold, little ears, I don't know why".

In 1945 "Plan of escape" is published. Emece publishers hire he and Borges to direct the detective collection "Septimo Circulo".

The following year, in collaboration with Silvina Ocampo he publishes "Los que aman, odian", a thriller; and with Borges "Un modelo para la muerte" and "Dos fantasias memorables". In 1948 "La trama celeste" a collection of short stories appears. In 1949 World War II ends. Bioy and Silvina travel to the States to meet Victoria Ocampo in New York. From there they go to France and then England, Switzerland and Italy. He then travels extensively and meets some of the best known writers: Octavio Paz, Andre Breton, Julien Green, Graham Greene, E.M. Forster,Vita Sackville-West, Alberto Moravia, Italo Calvino.

He re-reads poets: Manrique, San Juan de la Cruz, el Anonimo Sevillano, Lope de Vega, Fray Luis de Leon, Gongora, Quevedo, Lugones, Dario, and many more.

In 1952 his mother dies. He joins the writers who opposed Peron's dictatorship from the pages of the newspapers "La Nacion" "La Prensa" or the "SADE" (Society of Argentinian Writers).

In 1953 "El perjurio de la nieve" with the title of "El crimen de Oribe" is transposed into Argentinian cinema by the father and son team of Torres Rios & Torre Nilsson.

In 1954 his daughter Marta is born and he publishes "El sueño de los heroes". In 1955 he starts writing screenplays with Borges: "Los orilleros" and "El paraiso de los creyentes". Peron's government is ousted from power. Until 1962, the year in which his father dies, Bioy Casares reads and publishes incessantly. He starts photography and publishes "El lado de la sombra", for which he wins the Second National Prize of Literature (1963). In 1967 he publishes "El gran serafin" and continues his collaboration with Borges. "The invention of Morel" is produced by French TV. In 1968 "SUR" collection publishes his comedy "Siete soñadores". "La otra aventura", a series of essays, appears. The following year he publishes "Diary of the War of the Pig" and he and Borges write the screenplay "Invasion", later directed by Argentinian Hugo Santiago. In 1970 he is awarded the First National Prize of Literature for "El gran serafin".

During a vacation in Mar del Plata, he writes a comedy "La cueva de vidrio" and publishes "Breve Diccionario del Argentino exquisito" under the pseudonym of Javier Miranda. Diana, the dog that will be his model for "Sleep in the sun" enters his house. The book is published in 1973 and in 1975 he receives the Grand Honour Prize of the SADE. Several of his short stories are produced for the Argentinian and Spanish TV.

In 1978 he publishes "El heroe de las mujeres" and in 1979 many of his stories are produced by RAI TV in Italy. That same year, his sister in-law Victoria Ocampo dies in Buenos Aires. She leaves the legacy of the "SUR" collection, her houses – now public museums – and a life devoted to bring the best of culture to Argentina.

From there on he publishes intensely and his works are shot for film and TV. Numerous essays and theses about his novels and short stories are published by American and European Universities.

Among other prizes, he is decorated in 1981 with France's Legion d'honneur and in 1984, Italy gives him the Mondello Prize for best foreign author translated into Italian. To this follows the Esteban Echeverria Prize and Konex Prize for best novelist in Argentina.

After his last books "La aventura de un fotografo en La Plata" and "Historias desaforadas", he continues to write on a daily basis in Buenos Aires, where he lives with his wife Silvina Ocampo.

BIOY CASARES

BUENOS AIRES, 1987

Borges often said that despite their difference in age, Adolfo Bioy Casares was his teacher. A remark that is born out with the passing of time. In his long list of novels and short stories, Bioy Casares' vision deals with sinister scientific experiments, genetics, and the transformation of reality in space and time. Towards them he conveys a biting, ironic sense of humour that surfaces as a harsh critique of the contemporary world. Nevertheless, he always has tenderness and hope for today's man, surrounded by forces that threaten to push him towards a collective suicide.

Thoughts flashed through my head as I entered the substantial old building on Posadas street in Buenos Aires. How many times must Borges have slowly walked into this place? All the writers and artists, both Argentinian and foreign who must have taken the short trip in the elevator... all the friends and personalities who must have rung this bell, and waited in the austere, elegant hall. And to how many strangers must this smiling woman have said, "Come in please, Mr. Bioy will join you soon".

We enter the living/reception area, and she disappears. My eyes dart about. The room is long and high ceilinged. Flowers, and Silvina Ocampo's drawings and paintings are dotted around. Bookshelves filled with hundreds of books line the walls. Portraits of family and friends are casually displayed on the shelves too. At the end of the room is a long corridor. Another woman appears holding a big dark dog on a short leash. She smiles, the dog looks over suspiciously, and they disappear through the door I entered. Finally I see a silhouette coming along the corridor. It is unmistakeably Bioy Casares. He hardly seems to touch the

floor as he walks quickly along. Opening the double doors wide,
he greets me, smiling. Dressed like an English squire, he invites
me into his study.

Down the corridor to the left we enter the spacious, bright
room. Big windows look out over the old park – the one from my
childhood, with the magnificent rubber trees. The parquet floor,
the comfortable black leather sofas and a small coffee table, make
up an intimate living space. There are several tables to the side.
Long book shelves, family photos and piles of books and magazines scattered on the floor.

Bioy remembers my grandmother Lia Sansinena, and
praises her as "one of the most beautiful women in Buenos Aires".
He talks about my grandfather Pepe Galvez, as a pioneer importer
of cars to Argentina – a surprise to me – and a few days later he
shows me photographs of part of his family with mine. From
there on, everything went as if I had known him for ages. The first
interview nevertheless, started with the respectful form of the
"usted". After a few days we comfortably switched to the more
familiar "vos". The transition was so cordial and friendly, that I
almost lost sight of the writer Bioy Casares.

His way of talking, intimate, measured, respectful, could at
first sight seem, perhaps vulnerable. It is only a fleeting impression. As he becomes passionate about certain issues, his loquacity
becomes emphatic, ironic and even impatient.

When he stands and walks about, his silhouette totally
changes. I've never known anybody quite like that. Face to face,
Bioy is leonine, vital and with a certain distant reserve. In profile,
he simply is another person. He would forgive me if I say he
appears a bit older, unprotected, and with an eagle shadow that
darkens him. But, it's just in profile. It appears and dissapears
with the same speed. For really, Bioy Casares gives the impression of what he is: a gentleman from a race – regretably so – on
its way to extinction.

When "The invention of Morel" was published in 1940, the
writer inaugurated for Argentinian literature –and many others
as well– a highly original concept and manner of narrating. A fact
proven by the many translations of the work. The novel is a love
story in different dimensions of time and space, and the terrifying
possibility of the immortality of "living images". Speaking of the
plot, Borges reminds us in the prologue that "it wouldn't be
imprecise or hyperbolic to qualify it as perfect".

The ones that follow, principally "Plan of escape" and "La trama celeste" place the reader in the center of a carefully construted plot. Like a precise and mysteriously realistic machine.

Later on, and perhaps because of his taste for the thriller and the fantastic, the work of Bioy Casares contemplates both. And even more: the rational exploration of fantasy in the apparently trivial.

In his short stories, the Argentinian man in the street will appear portrayed without sentimentality nor concessions to his smallness. Nevertheless, he will be protected by the author in his everyday virtues, specially love and friendship.

Many books came out of his long friendship and collaborations with Borges. For example, there were fantastic thrillers, with the pseudonym H. Bustos Domecq and B. Suarez Lynch (honoring their ancestors) among the best of the genre.

Many of his stories were taken to film and television, if not always with the deepest satisfaction of the author. Among them: "El crimen de Oribe" based on "El perjurio de la nieve" by Argentinian directors Torres Rios and Torre Nilsson; "La guerra del cerdo (an adaptation from "The diary of the Pig War") by Torre Nilsson; "The invention of Morel" by French and Italian TV; "Cavar un foso" and "El atajo" for Argentinian TV.; "En memoria de Paulina" -one of his best short stories- for Spanish cinema directed by Braso; many short stories for RAI (Italian Broadcasting & TV) in 1979, with others in preparation.

Bioy Casares complained about one of the film versions of "The invention of Morel". "It lacked human warmth. It's very difficult" he adds "not to be boring when the main character is constantly in a state of awe and perplexity. He seems a bit of an idiot".

Bioy Casares is ceaselessly active continuing to write everyday, with the same vigour as when he started his career. The recognition of his work in Argentina and abroad, principally in Europe -in the form of all manner of prizes- places him among the finest living writers today. This prestige, slowly building in North America -English is the language into which he has been translated the least- will prove its solidity in time, as with all classic literature.

* * * * *

Galvez: Bioy, how has your childhood and country life influenced your work as a writer?

Bioy C.: That is not easy to explain but...let's try. Undoubtedly the country is one of the most real parts of the world for me. The country, plus the city of Buenos Aires. I have written many things about the city of Buenos Aires and I have written "Memoria sobre la Pampa y los Gauchos", which some generous people say, is the best of what I've written on the country. Critics however said that I was spending my life searching for gauchos that I couldn't find.It was ugly. It was a sarcastic synthesis of what I was saying in the book, but a bit stupid at the same time. My book tries to be an authentic hommage because it wants to be true. I think that continuous exaggerated hommages distort what they try to exalt. I have tried to write about the gaucho truthfully, showing all the misconception attributed to him and how nonetheless, he survived.

Galvez: You mention, precisely in that essay, how difficult it is sometimes to find our gaucho.

Bioy C.: Yes. Well, every Argentine who has spoken about the gaucho, from Vincente Lopez on , says that the gaucho disappeared 60 years ago. Which is to say, everyone places him in his childhood. Even I refer to the gaucho of my childhood, 60 or 65 years ago, when I'm not paying attention. Apart from that, I have been postponing a novel —one has that lazy side that employs us diligently in the most trivial matters, which are the most easy to handle. I have the idea of writing a novel that takes place in the country; the title will be: "El Fondo del Campo" ("The End of the Land"). You can tell the Canadians that in Argentina the end of the land is simply the end of each property. One says: I'm going to the end of the land...

Galvez: The limit...

Bioy C.: Yes. As the estancias used to be huge, and some of them still are, it is not an inappropriate name. And I believe it's quite pretty don't you?

Galvez: It's a very good title.You also wrote something, in the essay we were talking about, that seems absolutely precise to me. When you talk about the character Mendiville, you say that he uses "that delicate variety of emphasis which consists in saying less than what it is".

Bioy C.: That's right. Yes, it's true.

Galvez: I believe the English call that understatment.

Bioy C.: Understatment, precisely. Well (laughs)...in that, the gauchos are similar to the English. (laughs)
Yes, for example, when one goes horseback riding and the horse is walking, the gaucho goes to the extreme of saying the opposite thing. One decides, for instance, to gallop and they say: should we go slowly? (laughs). But to go slowly means to gallop...

Galvez: There are many other interesting things in that essay. For instance the gaucho's use of the language. You speak of his "precise vocabulary: that archaic, precise tone, that personal distinction". That character seems to invade the country. How do you compare it to the man in the city?

Bioy C.: The city is invaded by novelty, including idiomatic novelties.Luckily enough, these take time getting to the country. This reminds me of what Pedro Henriquez Urena told me one day when he was leaving this house. We were waiting for the elevator and he said: "To write well one has to think how a countryman would say it, an eloquent countryman of course. I think it's good advice because it means: let's eliminate fashionable language; what seems amusing to us because it is in the ambience, and let's limit ourselves to words that have survived for a long time; because if they had, it means they had a reason for being. It means they were "fostered".

Galvez: That they are classics.

Bioy C.: Yes, they are classics. The fact the︵ have been with us for long shows that.

Galvez: Because there is sometimes a certain laziness in thought processes...

Bioy C.: Of course.

Galvez: ...people tend to express themselves with slogans or made-up phrases.

Bioy C.: Yes, that's true. And also with neologisms; let's say pretensiously cultured words that hide a poverty of thought.

Galvez: Bioy, do you agree with what Octavio Paz said about your theme in stories and novels, not being cosmic but metaphysical?

Bioy C.: Well...I believe he is right. But...that statement exceeds my possibilities...(laughs).

Galvez: What I was aiming at is the "why of the writer". Did you choose it or did you feel chosen to write?

Bioy C.: Neither one nor the other. (laughs) I've always thought that one has to be deliberate in life. One has to believe in one's criteria and follow them, because there is no other compass. And because of that, one should try to choose good criteria and cultivate intelligence. But...I also believe that one should be modest. I have had many trials and things -good and bad- in my life, that happened despite my criteria. I wanted to be, and was, a good sportsman. And probably, what I wanted to be was world champion...

Galvez: In tennis?

Bioy C.: Well, tennis had a lot to do with it, yes. I have played tennis for almost 40 years. I believe I was a good tennis player. A good tennis player among the mediochre, but nevertheless. I was ranked 8th or 10th in the Buenos Aires Club, which is the best here. That's enough.
But....when something moving happened to me, my reaction was to write. I was not exactly brilliant in my compositions at school. But, for example, if I felt in love with a girl and she didn't pay any attention whatsoever, I thought of writing something about it. I used to spoil my possibilities of being loved, taking everything very lightly; ther I wrote about it. I wanted to write a book about "the clown's heart" (laughs)...luckily I didn't, but it was a project.

Then somebody talked to me about thrillers. I had never read any, but nevertheless I wrote a little story called "Vanity or Terrifying Adventure". It was a thriller halfway between mystery and fantasy. All these happened without my knowing that 'literature' existed. I was told about those books; I liked the idea of detectives and wrote about that. But I didn't think about books, nor wanted to read them.

Then one day I discovered 'Literature'. It was at the age of 12 or 13, and I felt an extraordinary fascination. I spent my entire time reading and seeking it out, even in books that today I find horrible. But I needed 'Literature' and in big doses too. That's why I liked Joyce's Ulysses and Gabriel Miro -I couldn't read him today- and today I think that "Ulysses" as a book is a terrible failure. Joyce is a great writer who has not left any good books. He has left some good pages, but that is a big problem don't you think? Furthermore, I believe he had a terrible influence on 'Literature' written by people who have not read him...more or less like me and the thrillers...

Galvez: Why do you think Joyce had a terrible influence on literature?

Bioy C.: Because people started searching for originality. And I believe that is catastrophic. Originality is inevitably within each one of us and that's what is worthwhile.

Galvez: Unique.

Bioy C.: Unique...what I mean is, it's going to be good or bad; if the person is a fool he will be an original fool, but worthless; if intelligent and curious he will be good. But we are all different. And to be able to give that note of distinction is what we can or should do, and nothing else. But you can't search for it. Searching for authenticity in oneself, if we have sufficient elements to find it and express it, will probably lead to original works that should be read, that deserve the reader's attention.

Galvez: Some critics like to impose 'fashions' on certain writers. Do you think Joyce had to do with that?

Bioy C.: Yes, he was introduced as fashionable, because well... he wrote to be in fashion; he was in vogue, and be, all that "modernity" and being in the "vanguard", seems to me to be a catastrophe. You can add Picasso and Braque, if you like, so the whole of Canada condemns me. (laughs) What can you do?

Galvez: Ludwig Zeller, a Chilean poet and friend of mine in Toronto, always says that Picasso destroyed the human figure in painting.

Bioy C.: Of course. Well, I can tell you that in "La Invencion de Morel" ("Morel's Invention"), the protagonist enters a place called "The Museum", which is a big house where he is going to live peacefully.He has to break chairs, things, and modern paintings to be able to survive.

I always think that those modern museum directors, show their insensibility because not only are they the directors but also live together with those things...

Going back to your original question; I read a lot; I wrote a lot and here you see me...writing. Writing from morning to night.

Galvez: And how did you read? Systematically, with some guidance?

Bioy C.: No, I didn't have any guide. One day I was reading "Introduction to Literature" for school and I read some poems that I liked and I don't know...I felt a fascination. I started to read voraciously, that's why I wrote so badly..I read everything I could, I played tennis, rugby, whatever, everyday, and I wrote everyday too...! (laughs)

Galvez: I was going to ask you about that. You are a man who practically had everything. You were the envy of many Argentinians; a good sportsman, a friend of Julio and Charlie Menditeguy (sporting phenomena in Argentina)...How did you manage to get on with your career and not be sidetracked, specially with the advances of women? (laughs)

Bioy C.: One day when we were having dinner at one of those Book Chamber meetings, I told Silvina Bullrich (Argentinian writer) that I played tennis everday; she said that I did everything, everyday...(laughs)

Galvez: Well then you must have had an extraordinary sense of order...

Bioy.: No. It was voracity. An extraordinary voracity. And so I wrote really terrible books. The worst books in the world. And I did them at the reader's expense. So now I owe them a double effort. I feel I am in debt to them; I gave them those horrible books. But in a way it was undoubtly, a good learning experience.

I published about six terrible books before "Morel's Invention" and left about ten or twelve novels unfinished. Some of them very long. Some, for example, I reached page 560...

Galvez: Are they all useless?

Bioy C.: Oh yes, totally useless. (laughs) If there is someone who would like to do something with them, it's at his own risk. But no, it couldn't do anyone any good to read them. Some say that you are equal to the food you take in. If they read them, they will become horrible writers afterwards...(laughs)

Galvez: Bioy, I didn't know you were a photographer. I was reading a book by Ricardo de La Fuente Machain about La Recoleta, and there were a lot of your photographs...

Bioy C.: Yes. For about ten years I photographed a lot too. Then I left it because...I thought you couldn't do both things: write and shoot...

Galvez: It is a passion...and talking about photography we could talk about another passion: cinema.

Bioy C.: Yes, of course. But about the La Fuente Machain book you mentioned...I thought the book wasn't very good; well, I've been unjust – and this happened to me many times – I've frivolously rejected certain things. But reading the book again, I think it's excellent; I hope the photographs are as good as the text.

Galvez: They are very good. The only thing is that the edition I saw could have been better printed...(laughs)

Bioy C.: Yes, the printing is not excellent, it is very Argentinian...(laughs)

Galvez: So, cinema is another of your passions...

Bioy C.: Yes, very early we tried with the Menditeguy brothers and with Drago Mitre, to make a film...but when we developed the film it was blank and we never found out why...(laughs)

Galvez: Did you have the cameras?

Bioy C.: Yes, yes. With a splendid Pathe baby machine...

Galvez: But you wrote for cinema; you did scripts..."Los Orilleros" with Borges...

Bioy C.: Well yes. We did those screenplays with Borges, when we didn't know how to write for cinema. So they came out like reading material; terrible as scripts. All the characters were uttering pared-down phrases...really intolerable if they're not said with humor or if the action doesn't have an extraordinary intensity to soften them. The actors look like children reciting someone else's text. Ridiculous. It was our mistake, Borges' and mine.

Galvez: But you both felt a passion for films...

Bioy C.: Yes, yes...

Galvez: Would you both have liked to direct? Or was it only writing?

Bioy C.: No. I don't think Borges or I thought about directing, because we soon discovered that we were bad leaders. I've told the story many times of when I was captain of a football team. We didn't play any games because I couldn't get together a group challenge. So I did the easiest thing there was: we continued to play among ourselves every day...(laughs) I've never been good for that kind of thing, neither was Borges. We were like shoe-makers doing their homework. We knew how to write and nothing else. Borges learned to speak because he lost his sight, and he had to look to that for...

Galvez: A compensation...
Bioy C.: A compensation of course, and without putting down the heroic way he overcome the illness. As he once told me: "It is easier to speak when one doesn't see the faces of the people listening; waiting for what one's going to say..." It is easier because it's like pure thought...

Galvez: Yes.

Bioy C.: ...instead, the face waits for an intelligent answer and you feel you're not really giving enough. Well...it's discour-aging or at least perturbing.
The first Borges' conference was when he was very close to someone reading it. He couldn't give it; he was too nervous to give it himself.

The same thing happened to me the first time I spoke on radio. I was seated with the microphone here, and I had the vivid impression that it was going to be difficult to remain seated; I thought I was going to slip and fall onto the floor. They are grotesque things but...the imagination can be mesmerizing...

Galvez: What did you think about the film "Diario de la Guerra del Cerdo" ("The Pig's War Diary"), based on your novel and directed by Torre Nilsson? (Argentine Director)

Bioy C.: I prefer not to talk about it. I love Torre Nilsson, he was a dear friend, very intelligent. When we talked about films with him, I felt he was a professional; but I thought the film he did was really disastrous...

Galvez: I thought so too...

Bioy C.: How could one not think so! If you thought it was good, I don't think we could continue talking...(laughs)
I've been lucky enough to be away when many good or bad things, based on my work were done. For example, most of the prizes given to me were given while I was away. I was in Paris when the SADE (Argentinian Society of Writers) gave the Honour Prize; and when I was given the Grand Prize of Literature. So when the "Pig's War Diary" opened in Buenos Aires, luckily I was not around; I didn't have to hide the suffering in my face. But I came back and it was still running in Buenos Aires. So I went to see it at the Broadway theatre. During the first three or four minutes I said to myself: "My God, what luck! They've made a film that can entertain an audience for a while". After six or seven minutes it was a catastrophe. Some young people in front of me were laughing. Not because the film was funny. They were laughing at the film. I felt the same way and suffered. I was upset at being part of something like that. Please don't say this...I love Beatriz (Beatriz Guido/Argentinian writer; Torre Nilsson's wife) very much...

Galvez: But in the end it wasn't really up to you...

Bioy C.: No, I'm not responsible. But Beatriz loves Torre Nilsson very much and he loves her. So, apart from that, I don't like to tred on my friends' feelings. We live in a difficult-enough world, and the least one could do is to be a friend of our friends...

Galvez: If you had to choose another profession, would you choose cinema?

Bioy C.: Oh no. But I love films. For example, I stopped going to the cinema for a while. I see films on cable TV and I'm very pleased. But I'm the most happy in the cinema theatre. This doesn't mean that I don't walk away annoyed sometimes when films are bad. But I like it very much and I believe there have been some splendid films made. Memories of my life are films...it's one of the arts that I hold nearest...

Galvez: Novel and film are very close aren't they?

Bioy C.: Of course! Very close. Novels and dreams too. And I'm very lucky to have a double life, during the day I live awake and I dream at night. I dream good, amusing things. Sometimes I dream in the third person. I'm seeing a story. So it is a little daily adventure that makes life worthwhile...the life of dreams.

Galvez: You once said: "Not to be the first in...

Bioy C.: But...(laughs) why do you know everything I've said...?

Galvez: (laughs)...well, I've done some homework...

Bioy C.: No, no, it's all right, on the contrary, I'm just joking...

Galvez: All right...you said: "Not to be the first ones in taking the new nor the last ones in disregard the old..."

Bioy C.: Alexander Pope said that, really. Do you know what happened with Alexander Pope and Ezequiel Martinez Estrada? (Argentinian writer) Martinez Estrada was a very intelligent man but solidly ignorant. He started writing a History of World Literature...and so...his friends helped him a bit. He made synthesis of Pope and Poe that unified them as Edgar Allan Pope...(laughs) Afterwards I told him that there was a biography of Johnson by Boswell. It was a revelation to him. He didn't read it probably, but at least he knew it existed.

Galvez: After many years of absence, last time in Buenos Aires I noticed a certain decadence in everyday language. You say that our way of talking is "moderate and of good tone". Is it like that now?

Bioy C.: Probably...but I'm talking about the language I knew as a boy. Because in a way everybody stays fixed in their youth...(laughs)

Remember the question about the gauchos; the gauchos disappeared 60 years ago...and one wants them to stay as you remember them. But I believe people used to speak fairly well here...

Galvez: How do you see it today?

Bioy C.: Not very well, undoubtedly. Worse than the way the Spanish speak. I don't think they speak badly there. It's funny, but they used a great number of "galicismos" (Gallicism). They pretend they cared about speech. They used to be like policemen pointing out gallicisms. It was an absurd obsession, because after all, language is a means of communication and should grow with the acceptance of words from everywhere. But now they have gone to the other side and have an excessive number of gallicisms and badly assimilated anglicisms.

Galvez: Then you think language changes daily?

Bioy C.: Yes, everyday. And then there are moments that are quite disagreable. Sometimes one recovers later on. Look, I have the impression that here, for example, some years ago language became overcrowded with horrible, absurd preciosities. That's why I wrote that "Breve Diccionario del Argentino Exquisito" (Brief Dictionary of the Exquisite Argentine) but I believe that fashion has lessened. I don't think I influenced that, but there was a reaction to it.

Galvez: Perhaps you had a lot to do with that, because you caught people's attention...

Bioy C.: Well, maybe I caught attention, but a lot of people complained and made fun of it. Fine. Now they try not to fall into that kind of nonsense. They won't loose that habit of adorning language completely, because after all that is the kind of writing they are able to do. It is somewhat, uncultivated people who have not given much thought to the language, and feel they're writing "literature"...

Galvez: That they are creating "Great Literature"...

Bioy C.: ...yes, "Great Literature" because they put in an unusual word here and there. That's the way they come out!

Galvez: Yes, in the end it's a terrible kind of pedantry...

Bioy C.: Well...I wouldn't say terrible, it's rather comic, modest pedantry. (laughs)

Galvez: I believe Psychoanalysis has also been deadly.

Bioy C.: Terrible! We should give thanks to Psychoanalysis and Sociology for a horrible language (laughs) don't you think? One sees that people look for precision in them. They don't want to say "el piso" (floor/apartment) because they fear it will mistake "apartment" for "floor". And so they use "planta", for example...

Galvez: And "planta" has the danger of being mistaken...

Bioy C.: Yes, of being mistaken for the kind of plant...(laughs) yes, that's why it goes on ad infinitum...

Galvez: When I arrived and was told that the neighbourhood starting in Callao and Santa Fe, towards the botanical gardens, is called "Villa Freud"...

Bioy C.: Yes, and...here there is an Analyst for every beard...(laughs) Don't take it personally...

Galvez: Bioy, talking about modern fantastic Literature...

Bioy C.: Just as we have the right to complain about Analysts, undoubtedly future generations will complain about Borges and Bioy and some others (laughs), because...fantastic literature will be a calamity by that time, don't you think?

Galvez: Why do you think so?

Bioy C.: Because things become a bit unbearable, when they start to be fashionable. A bit of fantastic literature was good; a lot of fantastic literature...

Galvez: Do you think we'll go back in that sense? That we live through periods, like spirals, touching similar points with different approaches..?

Bioy C.: It is inevitable, yes...Life is very short, but not so short that one cannot repent of the things one has proposed...(laughs). Because as Benavente said: "Blest are the disciples, they are our errors". With time one starts to say : "My God, could I write a psychological novel?" So...(laughs) one is in the middle of all this, fantastic things spring up...what can you do...?

Galvez: It's inevitable. Perhaps it has to do with Argentina too; a certain way of being, or perhaps with Buenos Aires...

Bioy C.: Yes, it's inevitable. Perhaps it's Buenos Aires. Or maybe reality itself. I think that with time, Government will have to create places where people can escape, because...it'll either be escapism or death...

Galvez: Politics is a theme that you hardly touch. How do you see what has happened lately in Argentina?

Bioy C.: What happened before was atrocious. I thought it was very good that the Peronists were removed because they were a calamity. But the ones who came afterwards surpassed them by far. It was right that they fought against the guerrillas and won. But the Mazorca (torture methods in old Argentinian history) methods are atrocious. The tortures are unforgivable and I don't believe in the efficiency of such things. It is obvious they have created a lot of resentment. And if the ones in power today, satisfy their vengeance; that resentment will continue and the country will end up as two vengeful Mafia families.

Galvez: On the other hand there seems to be no alternative. If Alfonsin is not there, who will be?

Bioy C.: Undoubtedly there is no alternative. And the hope that the country would grow up to be better educated; that it learns how to think better, seems very difficult at the moment. If it wasn't for the example of more "civilized" nations, we couldn't even believe in the possibility. Without trying to ressemble Goebbels, I see things called "culture" that are painful...(laughs) but one shouldn't joke about such things, culture is our only hope.

Galvez: Yes, because it comes from education. And that's why I suspect we are not going to see it. It starts in primary school...

Bioy C.: Yes. And it goes very slowly. It also seems that to win elections or to govern, they think more about the party interests and the elections than the country. I don't see they spend much time thinking about the country. The other alternative are military governments, but they have not had better results...

Galvez: They have been our national evil.

Bioy C.: Yes, incredible.

Galvez: Bioy, in you short story "La obra" (The play) you say...

Bioy C.: One has to be careful with what one says, because as Conan Doyle said "One should never confuse the maker with the doll". He says "place well in the tentacles of your brain, that the doll and her creator are never the same". He plays with the rhyme. I often make my characters say things that are contrary to my way of thinking...

Galvez: Yes. It's like rehearsing for cinema and telling an actor to improvise. It could be a fatal error because the actor improvises as himself and not from the character's persona...But I refer to your phrase "perhaps I'm not high up nor down below, I'm comfortable somewhere in the middle, in my opinion it's more decent".

Bioy C.: Yes, I believe that. There is a certain cheapness in success.

Galvez: But, is it necessarily like that? Couldn't being modest and succesful coincide?

Bioy C.: Of course they can. I'm not saying it is absolutely like that. But I believe it sounds better to say that, especially in a story. The narrator of the story is speaking. If I wanted to make him appear ridiculous, he could have said: "I mean to write a master piece so that everyone can admire me and set me down in the bronze book of Argentinian glory". Well no. I have to lower the tone a bit, and that's why I put it that way. In reality I have all those ambitions...(laughs) as does anyone who writes. But I don't write for my ambitions; I write to write well and to say exactly what I think and to be honest, and because I like writing...

Galvez: But then there is a noble vanity too. It is legitimate to be proud of one's good work...

Bioy C.: Yes, but I couldn't be totally proud of my work...

Galvez: Why not?

Bioy C.: No, no! Because I believe that everything happens a bit by chance...There are errors. I've never received a book of mine and been satisfied. I've always found that I said something wrong. Sometimes it seems I'm saying the contrary of what I mean...well, all errors are possible in human nature, and I always found them in what I do. So I would have to be a bit blind to be pleased with what I do. I can't blind myself enough. What I can affirm is that I always try to write the best possible way and that I can say: judge me for my books. With them I defend myself or fall. But I'm not as happy as to have that vanity satisfied; no, no, far from that. I'm proud of my demands more than my attainments.

Galvez: Somebody said that a film-and I believe it could apply to the novel-resolves itself in very different ways, in accordance with the life style, culture, etc. that each viewer or reader has...

Bioy C.: That's true.

Galvez: ...so that very thing, sometimes creates a rift between the writer and reader. It creates peculiar situations; for example: "I don't like what I write but this reader loves it, and I don't have the right to complain anymore..."

Bioy C.: All right. But for me the book is a machine that contains the text and the reader. The author disappears. I feel detached from my book until I have to correct a French translation, or there is a revision to be made. Then I read it again and correct it. But I stop thinking of what I've done, I only think of what I'm doing.

Galvez: It disappears.

Bioy C.: It disappears from my conscious mind so I can live in peace, don't you think?

Galvez: Haven't you gone through any of your books objectively?

Bioy C.: Not really. I have the two obvious reactions. I find sometimes I say something good and I'm pleased. Other times, I feel I slip up here and there...what can you do?

Galvez: Countries like Canada are enormously interested in Latinamerican literature...

Bioy C.: Yes, we are in fashion...(laughs) thanks to the polite weakness of world literature. So, here we are, writing as we always wrote while in other countries they are writing a bit below par.

In my travels I've seen that writers have lost...faith. I have the impression that professors and critics have watered literature down, and with their deadly influence, fiction writers seem to believe that the potential of imagination is exhausted. That to be original, variations are all that is left. I don't believe anyone can write like that. In my little writer business, I still believe in originality. When I think I have an original story, I propose it. It is risky for me and my readers. If I'm mistaken we'll both pay the price. But I naively keep writing about what seem to be attractive ideas. They don't appear to be able to do that anymore in Europe. They think in terms of: "well, this has been done already let's try something else". No, that cannot be. I believe it is also the disgrace of seeing oneself within the "History of Literature". The idea of the History of Literature is contrary to literary creation.

Galvez: Because it transforms itself into laboratory literature...

Bioy C.: Of course! And because then you have the influences, consequences...No, no..! Let's act...

Galvez:...with something that has to do with life...

Bioy C.: With life...completely so.

Galvez: And well, perhaps these are symptoms...because European vitality is a bit...

Bioy C.: Yes, but that is something else. I don't know if one could compare the continent's life to one's own life. There has been a fashion in critical circles; a flourishing of university literature to pass exams; essays about this or that writer, that has transformed itself into a parasitic literature. And it grows and grows. Even though it doesn't have more scope than the professors who analyze it, it has to search for a market. It finds it. Gets published, and starts convincing people of something that is false: a world of bibliographies...

Galvez: A vicious circle...

Bioy C.: A closed and filthy circle that is doing a lot of harm. Furthermore, it affects writers, because it makes them write for the History of Literature. And it harms the readers because it makes them believe that literature is something tedious; a search for influences and relations, when literature is a beautiful game –as Bergman said speaking about theatre: "People believe in our game so much, that they give us precious theatres so that we can play in them." How wonderful is that the editors take our games seriously, publish them and send them round the world...! (laughs)

Galvez: It's a bit like the complaint of a Canadian painter, who said that many of his colleagues got their "inspiration" from the latest French and American art magazines.

Bioy C.: How awful...

Galvez: It is terrible because...it's like the end; like the "History of Academic Painting"...

Bioy C.: (laughs) Oh, that's good!

Galvez: But within Latinamerican literature, the Argentinian one undoubtedly carries enormous weight...

Bioy C.: When I was in Italy recently to receive a prize, I had the good fortune to see that the "Buenos Aires Club" was much more popular than the "Caribbean Club"...(laughs)...this was in Italy of course.

Galvez: Bioy, which writers do you prefer?

Bioy C.: You mean today or from any time?

Galvez: Any time.

Bioy C.: There are so many...it's difficult to say. Starting with Doctor Johnson and Boswell and Hume, and leaving England...Montaigne and Proust, so many...

Galvez: Of course there are a lot, but I was thinking more about authors who influenced you.

Bioy C.: Well, one has to see the authors one prefers and the authors who influence. The authors one doesn't totally approve of, are the ones who influence you the most. They influence for the good and the bad. I was influenced by Azorin and today I don't like him. I was influenced by Gabriel Miro and I don't like Miro. I was influenced by Joyce, I don't like Joyce; Jung...I don't like Jung! Conan Doyle, well, I believe there are better writers than Conan Doyle...

Galvez: And the national ones?

Bioy C.: I like Mansilla very much and re-read him often; I re-read the old Lopez (Vicente Fidel Lopez)...

Galvez: From Lucio V. Mansilla, do you mean..."Una incursion a los indios Ranqueles"? ("An incursion to the Ranquel Indians")

Bioy C.: "An incursion" yes. But also "Entre nous" and "Le causerie". "The memoirs" I like a lot...I find everything that Mansilla has written very pleasant. Then the memoirs of General Paz, I think are excellent. Of course we aren't going to forget Borges, Silvina, (Silvina Ocampo, Bioy Casares' wife), Peyrou, Vlady Kociancich...so many!

Galvez: Yes, there are so many. That's one of the things I keep saying to friends in Canada. Borges is undoubtedly the best known, but there are so many more excellent ones...

Bioy C.: In 1986, an academic from the Maxim Gorky Academy in Russia, came to Buenos Aires. He was writing the History of Argentinian Literature and told me he read our "gauchescos" (Gaucho writers): Hilario Ascasubi, Hernandez, Estanislao del Campo, and some other of my favourite authors. He said to me: "Well...but Argentina is the writer's country! (laughs) The Russian knew a lot about such things. Later on we were talking and Marquitos Roca, a friend of mine, dropped in to say hello. When he left I casually said: that's a man by the name of Roca". The Russian replied: "A descendent of General Roca? "Yes" I said. "General Roca, the 1880 Desert Campaign! When I get back and tell my wife, she'll die of envy! (laughs)...Seeing a descendent of him, what a marvel!"

Galvez: Bioy, was if difficult to write with Borges?

Bioy C.: No! It was the easiest thing in the world! At least it was for me, and I think it was also easy for him. The only risk of collaborating with Borges was his mental velocity, and the ease with which he focussed on everything.

Borges started to write and there he was, thinking what he was doing. To disgress for a moment, when I was studying Law, I often found I was thinking about something else. And that anguished me. Once, Larreta (Enrique Larreta, Argentinian writer) visited me in Alta Gracia (province of Cordoba) and I asked him if he used to read many novels. He said no, because he had so much imagination that after the first page he would start thinking of something else. It was then that I took the firm determination never to let that happen to me, (laughs) and to pay attention to what I was doing. My father on the other hand, used to say: "Think what you are doing". which is undoubtedly good counsel. Furthermore, I read a beautiful essay from Maeterlinck called "The Emerphel horses" which was the result of a disappointment he suffered. He thought some Emerphel horses could speak. He didn't discover that the trainer probably taught them to respond to certain stimuli and reflexes.But that doesn't invalidate two facts: first, that the essay is very beautiful, and then, that those horses managed that, because the trainer obliged them to pay attention. Paying attention is the secret of everything, the secret of intelligence. Animals and humans too, resist fixing their attention. Were they able to do that –Maeterlinck says– they could even talk. Well, perhaps not, but they certainly do marvellous things reacting to stimuli.

Borges was also a living example of how one can concentrate. He always did that and was ready to work. I would often say to him: "I have bad news Georgie, we have to write a letter". "Very good, how lucky we are, let's write the letter" he replied. He was always ready to do whatever was to be done.

Galvez: And when you told him: "Georgie we have to write a story...?

Bioy C.: Oh, he was enchanted...Once, while I was watching my daughter play with a friend, a story occured to me. Each would describe the doll in their hands to the other, when it was easier to just show it. That night I said to Borges: "I think we have a story. It's about someone who writes for the pleasure of describing, and not for the merit the description might have". That was the start of a character, a writer whose name was Bonavena, who finds originality in describing his table, his eraser, his pencil...(laughs) and he writes horrible books. Well, that was the first story of a series called: "Bustos Domecq Chronicles". And it is called "An afternoon with Ramon Bonavena". Borges accepted the proposal, delighted. We wrote that one and then many more. After six months of work, Borges said to me that he was always grateful I proposed that first story, for it helped him

forget a lost love. I didn't proposed the story for that reason of
course. But you see, Borges was always ready to work. Not in
just anything but in things that he liked.

Galvez: Because a collaboration like the one both of you
had,is not frequent in literature.

Bioy C.: No, it's not very frequent. It started when I was
asked to write a pamphlet for yoghurt. Borges was going through
a hard time economically, and they were paying 16 pesos the
page. Of course, that was much more than any newspaper or
magazine was paying. 16 pesos was a lot in those days. So we
did that pamphlet about yoghurt and we had great fun writing it.
After that, Borges told me he had a story. It was about a certain
Dr. Pretorious, a German during the war – of course we resented
the Germans – who killed children by playful methods. He would
make them sing and play until they died from exhaustion. He had
a vacation camp prepared. (laughs) Well, that could have been a
good story. We didn't write it but it was the seed for: "Six
problems for Don Isidro Parodi", "Chronicles of Bustos Domecq",
"New Stories of Bustos Domencq", "Model for death" and also
"Two memorable fantasies".

Galvez: Tell me the yoghurt anecdote, they say both of you
were alone in an estancia...

Bioy C.: Yes, we were in Pardo, in the country. It was
bitterly cold, the house was in bad shape and the only comfortable
place was the dining room. So, we wrote there, in front of the
fire that was still working, drinking strong cocoa mixed with
water.

Galvez: I was always curious about Borges' vehement
insistence he was not a believer. That insistence, seemed almost
like a game...

Bioy C.: (laughs) I'm not a believer either...

Galvez: But I noticed it because he asked for a Catholic
priest before he died in Switzerland...

Bioy C.: Well, is better to remain silent about those things.
How can one know about those last moments?
When I learned my father had cancer, I think I even prayed,
and I'm not a believer. But if I'm told that feeding a toad will stop
a person I love from dying, then I would feed the toad, don't you

agree? When one is threatened by an extreme situation, one does anything. Furthermore, what a dying person asks for, is it really his asking? Or is it the people surrounding him, asking? I don't know that. I don't know if one has the vitality in those moments to reject or discuss something with a priest, for example...

Galvez: It is always interesting to discuss with a priest.

Bioy C.: Yes. I remember Baler said to a priest once: "Enough sir, leave, I can't stand your style". (laughs)

Galvez: Were you ever a believer?

Bioy C.: I was a believer while I prepared for my first communion. And I was the unhappiest youngster in the world; because I thought I was going to go to hell; that the world was like the surface of a very fragile egg and that at anytime, a demon was going to catch me; and that there was an horrendous basement. The nuns convinced me of that...

Galvez: That was before your first communion?

Bioy C.: That was before. The day of my first communion I was with a friend of mine, Drago Mitre, who had his first communion with me, and he said: "I hope you didn't believe all those tales of heaven and hell..." "you're right" I said, and felt liberated, and from there on I was happy for the rest of my life...

Galvez: So, you never more...

Bioy C.: Never more. I was even a member of the Racionalistic Press Association. It was a society of English free thinkers, Wells and Bertrand Russell were the last ones they had.

Galvez: Speaking of Wells...what do you think of Chesterton...? (laughs)

Bioy C.: I think he is an excellent writer. But...he was mistaken...(laughs) No, seriously, he was an excellent writer. I always recomend "The life of Browning" to those who talk about Chesterton, because it seems a very beautiful life to me...

Galvez: Yes, Chesterton wrote magnificent things. He is reappearing now...

Bioy C.: Yes. It always happens that way. When a writer

dies, he also dies for the critics, and then he reappears. Because...there aren't that many good things in the world. In spite of what Cansino said: "there shouldn't be so many wonderful things". He couldn't stand so many beauties...If you want my definition of the masterpiece...I have to find it...

Galvez: Yes, sure, go ahead.

(Bioy gets up and searches through the big room. He goes over papers, piles of books and manuscripts. No success.)

Bioy C.: Sorry I couldn't find it. Let me try it by heart. A masterpiece is a work that leaves us a good memory. So good, that it makes us forget its weak parts. We always praise them, although we have condemned many famous books and something we have to admire. (laughs).

This doesn't mean that I believe literature is full of excellent things. But if I didn't believe in it, I wouldn't have written. Because what make me write, is my fascination for Eca de Queiroz, or Stevenson or the writer I was reading at the time...

Galvez: Melville...

Bioy C.: Of course, Melville, yes, he's so good...

Galvez: A little while ago I was in Nantucket and went to where he lived and to the Museum of the Whale...

Bioy C.: Oh yes, what a place that is...

Galvez: Incredible, isn't? The original of "Moby Dick" is there...

Bioy C.: Yes, so beautiful...

Galvez: Well, I think Borges always used to say that everything passed through New England, more or less...

Bioy C.: And it's true, it's true...

Galvez: Bioy, what about the contemporary Argentinians?

Bioy C.: Who do you mean? Young writers...?

Galvez: Fine, young writers.

Bioy C.: Well, there is Vlady Kociancich; there is

Soriano...he isn't bad at all Soriano, he's good; there is...who else? Marcelito Pichon Riviere perhpas; there is also Francis Korn, a friend of mine...(laughs)

Galvez: Perhaps she is...(laughs)

Bioy C.: I hope so...

Galvez: And as a writer Bioy, what infernos and what Paradises?

Bioy C.: (smiling) As writer what infernos and Paradises? Paradises...undoubtedly, good books. Good books, good women...(laughs), agreeable days, feeling well, bread, water...I've always thought that if I were condemned to bread and water, I would be happy; there's nothing that I like more than good bread and nothing I like more that tasty water. And infernos...the myths. Yes, the popular myths; those admirations for things that are not worthwhile...

Galvez: Gardel (Carlos Gardel, Argentinian world-famous tango singer) would be a kind of inferno?

Bioy C.: And why not. Not everything he has sung. He has sung somethings I like, but...

Galvez: The myths yes.

Bioy C.: The myths yes...and there are other tango singers that I liked more than him, my God, and female tango singers as well. I don't like his sentimental side.

Galvez: I think that is a misconception. It doesn't belong to Argentinians, as many people believe. It shows up specially, in bad Argentinian films. As the popular saying goes: "now for the tango and the violins..." (laughs)

Bioy C.: Yes, yes, of course.

Galvez: There is a good Argentinian film, which I saw in Toronto called "Man looking Southeast" that doesn't have those faults...

Bioy C.: I saw it, yes, I liked it...

Galvez: By the way, it mentions your book "Morel's invention"...

Bioy C.: Yes. It doesn't have those weaknesses. But I would say that the Americans share that kind of fault with us.

Galvez: Yes.

Bioy C.: We both do that. You also see it in novels, even strong ones, where they resort to: "when in doubt kill a baby". It seems that is a solution that works in many things. Extending "baby" to anything. It could be the granny also; or a noble animal, or whatever.

Galvez: People said that the Italian influence here, had a lot to do with it. But I believe it's something else...

Bioy C.: They do it much less in Italy, it seems to me...

Galvez: What happens is that they make more fuss about it, perhaps they're more spontaneous. But one prefers another style, for there are many varieties of Argentinians.

Bioy C.: Yes. One likes discretion...(laughs)

Galvez: But perhaps when one is in Toronto, among the most discrete, one misses Argentinian sentimentalism...

Bioy C.: (laughs) That's the way...

Galvez: Sometimes I feel Latin and that English order does me good. Perhaps if I went to Rome I would be totally lost, I don't know...

Bioy C.: Yes, but I don't see that the Romans are so lost, that's the funny thing. Because you see Italian cinema is much less superstitious than ours. In our cinema the film and viewer always share some kind of superstitious complicity. It makes them go and see it. They buy them with a sophism which they half believe, but they like to believe in. There is nothing like that in Italian films. They say whatever it is strongly. As you see for example in some Ettore Scola films, where the poor are horrible...(laughs)...and they don't care at all. The Italians are like that; they don't believe one defends the poor by making them "folkloric", ficticious, noble,...no. They present things in another way. One really wishes there weren't any poor people seen it this way.

Galvez: What about Argentinian cinema?

Bioy C.: It hurts me. There are exceptions, as everywhere.
But in general, I don't like it very much. I hope they'll make films
that correspond to our literature. Let's say it boastfully, since I
am a writer...

Galvez: Bioy, you have mentioned Lord Byron many times...

Bioy C.: Yes. I spend my life reading Lord Byron's letters.
And I like "Don Juan" and I like "Beppo". I think he saw that division
line very clearly: the things he wrote in the past, that he didn't like,
but was admired for; and "Don Juan" and "Beppo", which were
really good, but were not accepted by his contemporaries. And
of course his letters, which are wonderful, and make me furious
with the people who burned his memoirs. I'm sure they would
have been..."a joy forever"...(laughs)

Galvez: Yes. He has a quote on his dog's tomb, beautiful...

Bioy C.: Beautiful, yes...

Galvez: ...to his dog, Boatswain...

Bioy C.: ...yes...I remember...

Galvez: It is one of the most touching things...

Bioy C.: How was it?

Galvez: I won't remember it exactly, but I believe it was:
"Here lies the one who had beauty without vanity, strength without insolence, courage without ferocity, and human virtues without the vices...

Bioy C.: It is so beautiful...He also wrote something about his
daughter, didn't he? The daughter who died. He says he can go
to her but she can't go to him. She's gone...That quote about
Boatswain, is so good...

Galvez: Yes, I like Byron very much...

Bioy C.: How lucky. And then, what Byron says about the
"units" is very precise. When he speaks about his theatre, he says
it is theatre that is not for the theatre. It is theatre to be read,
and, he says, at least respects units. He says, on one side you have
the units and on the other the barbarians. I found rather extraordinary that the chief of the romantics would say that. Because
I don't believe one should respect the time units of 24 hours and

all that, but it's true that the more action is comprised, in time, in everything, the better stories develop. And you get better novels. It is a pragmatic matter.

Galvez: Perhaps there is a repetition of cycles. I don't know if Romanticism will come back, but it is a contrast to this mechanized era...

Bioy C.: Furthermore, they're the two possibilities: Classicism and Romanticism; they are always returning disguised in some way.

Galvez: Bioy, did the fact that you married Silvina Ocampo, who is a writer, influence your literature?

Bioy C.: No...Silvina influenced my literature by telling me not to continue law and to dedicate myself to writing, and nothing more than writing. In that sense yes, she saved me. She and Borges, they both told me the same.

Then I can add I'm very comfortable with writers. Silvina is really a writer in the true sense of the word. I mean: she sees the world as a writer and that for me has always been stimulating and comfortable. And well...I was always a friend of Borges; I've been friends with Peyrou, I'm a friend of Vlady Kociancich. Of course you can also find some of the most disagreable people in the world are writers. You have the vain ones, and it's uncomfortable to be friends with writers who write badly. Friendship makes one tell the truth...and how do you tell the bad writer: you write badly. I'm talking about adults, who keep publishing and publishing bad books after 30 years...That is a difficult friendship; because if one has to be silent about the most important thing a writer does, which is to write...But with writers one likes, it's very comfortable...

Galvez: Well, if there is true friendship and he is a writer, it's not that difficult to say: "this is not very good..."

Bioy C.: Yes, but when you don't like any of his work, it's horrible...

Galvez: (laughs) Yes, that friendship is almost impossible...
Could you have married someone who wasn't a writer?

Bioy C.: Oh yes...probably yes...

Galvez: So it wasn't important that she was...

Bioy C.: No. It was a lucky circumstance; because I carry everything to literature...perhaps I might have even told a non-writer, why don't you write a bit?...(laughs). But that's due to lack of imagination on my part.

I believe writing helps so much to live. It is like giving reality another room in which to place its things. Furthermore, you are seeing reality like something to be told in a story. It's like that all the time.

I have the impression that my mind is a kind of little cinema that is constantly working and entertaining me. I try to make it entertain everyone else.

That's why I don't have any intention of dying, because that is like shutting the curtain, isn't it? And since I write diaries and commentaries, when something happens to me, something ridiculous or a bad thing, I say to myself: how lucky! I have something good to write in the diary. Because it's more fun to write that, than to write about a success. A success is very difficult to handle and write about. Immediately you see the vanity coming out. That prize was won, etc. so what? Instead I was put in my place; this other thing happened...it's much more funny...

Galvez: Yes, because the theme of happiness is very boring.

Bioy C.: Yes, of course. I believe that is one of the things I have problems with. I have a clash with readers and analysts. They believe: Heavens! You must have been very sad to write that kind of ending. They don't realize that perhaps when I found that ending, I started laughing out of joy, because it was the appropriate ending to the story.

Writers are searchers of all kinds of characters, details, and situations.

Many times we write a story to get to an ending; but many times not. We depart from a situation. And we don't know what ending we are going to put in. And we feel miserable because we don't find it. And when we do find it, and perhaps it's a terrible tragic one, that day we are happy, we eat with appetite, we talk about it with other writer friends who are going to celebrate this. And then, in comes the reader who cries at that moment and thinks: how sad, how depressed Bioy must have been to write this. Well...No!!...(laughs) It was a moment of great vitality and joy! (laughs).

PRINCIPAL WORKS BY ADOLFO BIOY CASARES:

(Original title, year of first edition and publishing house. Unless otherwise noted, all originated in Buenos Aires, Argentina).

"Prologo" (1929, Editorial Biblos).
"17 Disparos contra lo porvenir" (1933, Editorial Tor) (Under the psuedonym of Martin Sacastru)
"Caos" (1934, Editorial Viau y Zona)
"La nueva tormenta o la vida de Juan Ruteno" (1935)
"La estatua casera" (1936, Ediciones del Jacaranda)
"Luis Greve, muerto" (1937, Editorial Destiempo)
"Antologia de la Literatura Fantastica" (1940, Sudamericana) (Collaboration with Jorge Luis Borges and Silvina Ocampo)
"Seis problemas para Don Isidro Parodi" (1942, Sur) (With Jorge Luis Borges under the pseudonym of H. Bustos Domecq)
"Los mejores cuentos policiales" (1943, Emece) (Selection and translation with Jorge Luis Borges)
"El perjurio de la nieve" (1945, Cuadernos de La Quimera)
"Plan de evasion" (1945, Emece)
"Los que aman, odian" (1946, Emece, Coleccion Septimo Circulo) (Collaboration with Silvina Ocampo)
"Dos fantasias memorables" (1946, Oportet y Haereses) (Collaboration with Jorge Luis Borges under the pseudonym of H. Bustos Domecq)
"Un modelo para la muerte" (1946, Oportet y Haereses) (Collaboration with Jorge Luis Borges under pseudonym of B. Suarez Lynch)
"La trama celeste" (1948, Sur)
"Prosa y verso de Francisco Quevedo" (1948, Emece) (Collaboration with Jorge Luis Borges selection)
"Las visperas de Fausto" (1949, La Perdiz)
"El sueño de los heroes" (1954, Losada)
"Los Orilleros" y "El paraiso de los creyentes" (Two screenplays in collaboration with Jorge Luis Borges) (1955, Losada)
"Poesia Gauchesca" (1955, Fondo de Cultura Economica, Mexico) (Collaboration with Jorge Luis Borges)
"Cuentos Breves y extraordinarios" (1955, Raigal) (Collaboration with Jorge Luis Borges. Anthology)
"Historia prodigiosa" (1956, Obregon S.A. Mexico)
"Guirnalda con amores" (1959, Emece)
"El libro del cielo y el infierno" (1960, Sur) (Collaboration with Jorge Luis Borges. Anthology.)
"Hilario Ascasubi, Aniceto el gallo y Santos Vega" (1960, Eudeba, Serie del Siglo y Medio) (Selection with Jorge Luis Borges)
"El lado de la sombra" (1962, Emece)
"El gran serafin" (1967, Emece)
"Cronicas de Bustos Domecq" (1967, Losada) (Collaboration with Jorge Luis Borges)
"La gran aventura" (1968, Galerna)
"Diario de la guerra del cerdo" (1969, Emece)

"Memoria sobre la pampa y los gauchos" (1970, Sur)
"Historias de amor" (1972, Sur)
"Historias fantasticas" (1972, Emece)
"Dormir al sol" (1973, Emece)
"Nuevos cuentos de Bustos Domecq" (1977, Ediciones Libreria La Ciudad)
        (Collaboration with Jorge Luis Borges)
"El heroe de las mujeres" (1978, Emece)
"Breve Diccionario del Argentino exquisito" (1978, Emece)
"La aventura de un fotografo en La Plata" (1985, Emece)
"Historias desaforadas" (1986, Emece)
"Paginas de Adolfo Bioy Casares seleccionadas por el autor" (1987, Celtia)

BIBLIOGRAPHY ABOUT ADOLFO BIOY CASARES:

Alazraki, Jaime: "Las Cronicas de Don Bustos Domecq". Revista Iberoameri
    cana, Mexico. No. 70, Enero 1970.

Anderson, Imbert, Enrique: "Historia de la literatura hispanoamericana, Mexico,
    Fondo de Cultura Economica, 1954 and 1957.

Armani, Horacio: "Entre el humor y la critica" in La Nacion, Buenos Aires, 14
    May 1967.

Bartholomew, Roy: "Cuentos breves y extraordinarios" in EL Hogar. Bs. As. 2
    March 1956.

Bastos, Maria Luisa: "Habla popular/Discurso unificador: "El sueño de los
    heroes de Adolfo Bioy Casares" in Revista Iberoamericana, No. 125, Oct,
    1983.
Bonet, Carmelo M: "La novela" in "Historia de la literatura argentina, Peuser,
    Buenos Aires, 1959.

Borges, Jorge Luis: Prologue to "La invencion de Morel", Losada, Buenos Aires,
    1940.

Borges, Jorge Luis: "La estatua casera", Sur, No. 18, Buenos Aires, 1936.

Borges, Jorge Luis: "Luis Greve, muerto", Sur No. 39 Dec. 1937.

Borges, Jorge Luis: "El sueño de los heroes", Sur No. 235, Aug. 1955.

Borinsky, Alicia: "Plan de evasion de Adolfo Bioy Casares: La representacion
    de la representacion". XVI Congreso del Instituto Internacional de
    Literatura Iberoamericana, Michigan, Aug, 1973.

Carella, Tulio: "Libro del cielo y el infierno" in Sur, No. 271. Jan. 1956.

Carrouges, Michel: "Les mondes insolites", Preuves, No. 23, Paris, 1953.

Carrouges, Michel: "L'invention de Morel" Monde Nouveau Paru, Geannee, No. 67, Paris, 1953.

Castagnino, Raul H.: "Otros caminos de la estilistica", Humanidades, Universidad Nacional de La Plata, 1960.

Cozarinsky, Edgardo: "Guirnalda con amores" in Sur, No. 261, Nov. 1959.

Cuneo, Dardo: "Presencia de la imaginacion con Adolfo Bioy Casares, Cuadernos Americanos, Mexico, 1946.

Chacel, Rosa: "Los que aman, odian" in Sur, No. 143, Sept. 1946.

Dumas, Norma and German Berdiales: "Dos opiniones" in Boletin del Instituto Amigos del Libro Argentino, Bs. As. No. 13, March 1956. "Los orilleros y El paraiso de los creyentes" in idem, idem, idem, Bs. As. No. 13. idem.

Eandi, Hector: "El sueño de los heroes", Boletin del Instituto Amigos del Libro Argentino, No. 9. Buenos Aires, 1955.

Etchebarne, Miguel D.: "Remembranza e incognita en El lado de la sombra" in La Nacion, 1963. Historia de un desaparecido" in La Nacion, 4 Oct. 1959.

Fevre, Fermin: "Las cronicas de Bustos Domecq" in El Cronista Comercial, Bs. As. 8 Feb 1967.

Garcia, German: "La novela argentina", Sudamericana, Buenos Aires, 1952.

Ghiano, Juan Carlos: "Dos cuentistas extraños: Bioy Casares y Glorla Acorta Ficcion, No. 11, 1958.

Goimard, Jacques: "Bioy Casares entre Stevenson et Robbe-Grillet" in Le Monde, 9 Aug. 1973.

Gonzalez Lanuza, Eduardo: "Antologia de la literatura fantastica", Sur, No. 81, Buenos Aires, 1941.

Gonzalez Lanuza, Eduardo: "Las palabras presuntuosas" in La Nacion, 6 Aug. 1978. La invencion de Morel" in Sur, No. 75, Dec. 1940.

Jitraik, Noe: "Historia prodigiosa" in Lyra, Bs. As. No. 186–188.

Jurado, Alicia: "El lado de la sombra" in Sur, No. 283, July 1963.

Kovacci, Ofelia: "Espacio y tiempo en la fantasia de Adolfo Bioy Casares" Facultad de Filosofia y Letras, Instituto Ricardo Rojas 1963.

Labarthe, Andre S. and Rivette, Jacques: "A conversation with Alain RobbeGrille,

New York, Film-Bulletin, V. 3, No. 2 (issue 43) March 1962. (Translated from Cahier du Cinema, No. 123)

Levine, Suzanne J.: "Guia de Adolfo Bioy Casares", Madrid, Editorial Fundamentos, 1982. Coleccion Espiral, No. 61.

Loprete, Carlos Alberto: "Cuentos breves y extraordinarios" (Antologia) in Ficcion, Bs. As. No. 3 Sept. 1956.

Loubet, Jorgelina: "Las maquinas celibes y La invencion de Morel" in La Nacion, 26 Sept. 1970.

MacAdam, Alfred J.: "El espejo y la mentira, dos cuentos de Borges y Bioy Casares" in Revista Iberoamericana, Pittsbourgh, No. 75, April-June 1971. Narrativa y Metafora: "Una lectura de La invencion de Morel" in XVI Congreso del Instituto de Literatura Iberoamericana, Michigan, Aug. 1973.

Maldavsky, David: "Las opciones y el azar en el universo narrativo de Bioy Casares. Un enfoque sintactico" in Nueva narrativa Hispano-americana, 2, New York, Adelphie University, 1972.

Mallea Abarca, Enrique: "Luis Greve, muerto" in Capitulo, Bs. As. .No. 3, Jan. 1938.

Martinez, Carlos Damaso: "La literatura fantastica". Desde sus comienzos a Bioy Casares". Bs. As. Centro Editor de America Latina. 1981.

Martinez J.L.: "Una novela fantastica de Hispanoamerica", Cuadernos Ameri canos, No. 2, Mexico, 1942.

Mastronardi, Carlos: "La trama celeste", Sur, No. 179, Buenos Aires, 1949.

Marcel Schneider: "Adolfo Bioy Casares. L'invention de Morel", La table ronde, No. 62, Paris, 1953.

Minguel, Maria Esther de: "Adolfo Bioy Casares. Historia prodigiosa" in Senales, Bs. As. No. 132, Sept 1961.

Milano, Paolo: "La triste allegoria della guerra al maiale" in L'Espresso, 4 April, 1971.

Molloy, Silvia: "Isidro Parodi, varios problemas para el traductor", in Sur, No. 312, Bs. As. May 1968.

Monges, Hebe: "El perjurio de la nieve" introduccion y notas. Bs. As. Ediciones Colihue, 1981. "La invencion de Morel", intro y notas. Bs. As. Ediciones Colihue 1981.

Olaso, Ezequiel de: "Seis problemas para Don Isidro Parodi" in Cuadernos del Congreso para la libertad de la cultura, Paris, No. 99, Aug. 1966.

Pagella, Angela Blanco Amores: "Problemas esteticos y humoristicos" in La Prensa, Bs. As. 23 July 1967.

Pages Larraya, Antonio: "Fantasia y prodigio" in La Prensa, Bs. As. 24 Sept. 1961.

Pichon Riviere, Marcelo: "Un modelo para el humor" in Revista Panorama, Bs. As. No. 212, May 1971.

Portuondo, Jose Antonio: "En torno a la novela detectivesca", La Habana, Ediciones Cuadernos Cubanos, 1946.

Rabassa, Gregory: "Los mejores cuentos policiales" in Revista Hispanica Moderna, New York, No. 4 Oct. 1954.

Reyes, Alfonso: "El deslinde", El colegio de Mexico, Mexico, 1944.

Robbe-Grillet, Alain: "Adolfo Bioy Casares. L'invention de Morel", Critique, No. 69, Paris, 1953.

Rodriguez Monegal, Emir: "La invencion de Bioy Casares" in Plural, No. 29 Feb. 1974. Dos cuentistas argentinos", in Clinamen, Montevideo, No. 3, July 1947.

Roggiano, Alfredo A.: "Adolfo Bioy Casares, en Diccionario de la literatura latinoamericana, Argentina, Union Panamericana, Washington, D.C., 1960.

Rosales, Cesar: "La invencion de Morel", in Sur, No. 179, Sept 1949.

Ruiz, Roberto: "Los orilleros. El paraiso de los creyentes", in Revista Hispanica Moderna, New York, Vol XXII, No. 3-4, July 1956.

Sabato, Ernesto: "Plan de evasion", Sur, No. 133, Buenos Aires, 1945.

Saiz, Victor: "Libro del cielo y del infierno" in Ficcion, Bs. As. No. 52 June 1971.

Schienes, Graciela: "Bioy Casares en un cuento de Cortazar" in La Gaceta Tucuman, 20 Nov. 1983.

Schneider, Marcel: "Adolfo Bioy Casares. L'invention de Morel" in La table ronde, No. 62, Paris, Feb 1959.

Schoo, Ernesto: "Los infinitos mundos de Adolfo Bioy Casares" in La Nacion, Bs. As. 21 June 1959.

Soto, Luis Emilio: "Bioy Casares y la literatura dirigida", Argentina Libre, Buenos Aires, Feb. 1941.

Soto, Luis Emilio: "El cuento" (XXV), en Historia de la literatura argentina, T 4, Peuser, Buenos Aires, 1959.

Tamargo, Maria Isabel: "El discurso de Adolfo Bioy Casares como   produc cion narrador, personajes, trama y lector". Ph.D. ponencias, John Hopkins University, Sept. 1975.

Torres-Rioseco, Arturo: "Nueva historia de la gran literatura hispanoamericana", T 2, Mexico, 1959.

Vidal Buzzi, Fernando: "Cuentos breves y extraordinarios", in Revista de Educacion, La Plata, No. 8 Aug. 1956.

Villordo, Oscar Hermes: "Genio y figura de Adolfo Bioy Casares", Bs. As. Eudeba, 1983.

Zum Felde, Alberto: "Indice critico de la literatura hispanoamericana", T 2, Mexico, 1959.

Agosti, Hector P.: "Cantar opinando", Editorial Boedo, Buenos Aires, 1982.

Armani, Horacio: "Las grietas de la realidad", sobre "El heroe de las mujeres, La Nacion, Buenos Aires, 1978.

Barrenechea, Ana Maria: "La expresion de la irrealidad en la obra de Borges", Paidos, Buenos Aires, 1967; "El conflicto generacional en dos novelistas hispanoamericanos: Adolfo Bioy Casares y Elena Portocarrero, Ocasional Papers, No. 18, New York University, and Textos Hispanoamericanos, Monte Avila, Caracas, Venezuela, 1978.

Barrera, Trinidad: "La invencion de Morel". "El gran serafin", Ediciones Catedra, Madrid, Spain, 1982.

Bullrich, Silvina: "El sueño de los heroes", La Nacion, Buenos Aires, 1969.

Butor, Michel: "Sobre Literatura", Seix Barral, Barcelona, Espana, 1967.

Campos, Jorge: "La magia en la realidad: Adolfo Bioy Casares", Insula, No. 365, Madrid, Spain, 1977.

Gallagher, David P.: "The novels and short stories of Adolfo Bioy Casares", Bulletin of Hispanic Studies, LII, 1975.

Gilio, Maria Esther: "Adolfo Bioy Casares", Clarin, Cultura y Nacion, Buenos Aires, April 1982.

Gomez, Carlos Alberto: "Adolfo Bioy Casares ensayista", La Nacion, Buenos Aires, Marzo 1969.

Kovacci, Ofelia: "Adolfo Bioy Casares ", Ediciones Culturales Argentinas, Buenos Aires, 1963.

Mangel, Alberto: "Plan de evasion" preliminary study, Editorial Kapelusz, Buenos Aires, 1974.

Monges, Hebe: "El perjurio de la nieve", Introduccion, notas y propuestas de trabajo, Ediciones Colihue, Buenos Aires, 1981.

Monges, Hebe: "La Invencion de Morel", idem, idem.

Muller, Martin: "Cuando los argentinos quieren ser exquisitos", Revista La Nacion, Buenos Aires, april 1978.

Paz, Octavio: "Corriente alterna", Siglo XXI Editores, Mexico 1967.

Pezzoni, Enrique: "Adversos milagros", selection of short stories of Bioy Casares. Monte Avila Editores, Caracas, 1969.

Rest, Jaime: "Las invenciones de Bioy Casares", Los libros, No. 2, Buenos Aires, 1969.

Roffe, Reina: "Adolfo Bioy Casares, sus laberintos y perjurios", Revista Siete Dias, Buenos Aires, Julio 1977.

Scheines, Graciela: "Los personajes de Bioy Casares: criaturas entre dos mundos", La Gaceta, Tucuman, Nov. 1981.

Tamargo, Maribel: "La invencion de Morel: lectura y lectores", Revista Iberoamericana, No. 96–97, Pittsbourgh, USA. 1976.

Vasques, Maria Esther: "Bioy Casares for export", interview. La Nacion, January, 1978. "Dialogo con lectores en la Feria del Libro". Idem, idem. March 1978.

JORGE LUIS BORGES

*B*orn on August 24, 1899 in Buenos Aires, Argentina. He was the son of Professor of modern languages Jorge Borges and Leonor Acevedo. At the age of 15 he travels with his family to Europe, and at the outbreak of war they settle in Switzerland where he finishes his secondary education. By that time he has already written his first short story "La visera fatal" and translated Oscar Wilde's "The Happy Prince" into Spanish.

In 1919-21 he travels around Spain and associates with the Ultraist literary group (Rafael Cansinos Assens, Guillermo de Torre, etc.) His first poem is published in the magazine "Grecia". In 1921 he returns to Argentina where he publishes the magazine "Prisma" with some friends. Next year he founds the literary magazine "Proa". In 1923 "Fervor de Buenos Aires", his first book of poems is published. He contributes to the literary magazine "Martin Fierro". In 1925 publishes his second book of poetry "Luna de enfrente" and his first book of essays "Inquisiciones". From 1926 to 1930 he publishes 2 essays "EL tamaño de mi esperanza" and "El idioma de los Argentinos". His third book of poems appears – "Cuaderno San Martin". In 1930 he publishes "Evaristo Carriego" and meets Adolfo Bioy Casares. They collaborate on various literary undertakings during the next three decades. He continues to write essays and film criticism. In 1935 "Historia Universal de la Infamia" appears. It is a collection of some of his first efforts at writing prose fiction. When his father dies in 1938, Borges is appointed librarian of a small municipal Buenos Aires library. He continues to write numerous short stories.

In 1941 appears "El jardin de los senderos que se bifurcan", an anthology of his short stories and in 1944 "Ficciones", his most celebrated collection of stories.

In 1945 when the Peronist era begun in Argentina, his sister Norah and mother are detained in a public demonstration against the regime. The Argentinian Society of Writers (SADE) creates the Grand Prize and awards it to him.

In 1946 he signs various anti-peronist declarations with other intellectuals. The government transfers him from his job at a library to the position of Municipal Inspector of chicken and rabbits. He resignes and to support himself starts giving conferences and talks.

In 1949 he publishes "El Aleph" and achieves national recognition. These are stories of fantastic speculation often masquerading as essays or taking form of adventure tales and detective stories. His narrative skills are compared with those of Edgar Allan Poe and Franz Kafka, whose stories he translated into Spanish.

In 1954 the first book of literary criticism dedicated exclusively to his work and its influence appears: "Borges y la nueva generacion" by Adolfo Prieto. In 1955 Peron and his government fall. Borges is appointed Director of the National Library in Buenos Aires. Next year he takes the chair of English and North American Literature at the University of Buenos Aires.

In 1961 "Antologia personal" is published. It's Borges's selection of his own preferred prose and poetry. He shares with Samuel Beckett the $10,000 International Publishers' Prize. In that same year he leaves for the University of Texas to lecture on Argentinian literature. In 1962 he lectures at universitites in the eastern United States; then returns to the University of Buenos Aires to teach a course in Old English. It is the year of his first book published in English: "Ficciones" (Grove Press) and a selection of his best prose writings, "Labyrinths" (New Directions).

From there on his international reputation grows constantly. He is awarded many prizes. In Buenos Aires, the President of Italy, Giovanni Gronchi awards him the title of Commendatore. The French government gives him the Commandeur de L'Ordre des Lettres et des Arts. A film directed by Argentinian Rene Mugica based on his short story "El hombre de la esquina rosada" is released in Buenos Aires.

In 1963 he leaves for a brief tour of Europe (Spain, Switzerland, France, and England). In England he lectures on English and Latin American literary topics. He travels later to Colombia to lecture and receives an honorary degree from the University of Los Andes. Meanwhile he occasionally publishes poetry in Argentinian newspapers. Borges who has been troubled by his sight for many years, now becomes blind. He dedicates much of his energy to his classes at the University.

In 1965 he receives the KBE (Knight of the British Empire) from Great Britan; Florence's Golden Medal of the IX Poetry Prize; from Peru the "Orden del Sol" award; then in collaboration with Maria Esther Vasquez he publishes "Literaturas Germanicas Medievales" and "Introduccion a la literatura inglesa".

In 1966 he re-assesses his poetic works (1923-66). He receives the Annual Literary Award of the Ingram Merrill Foundation in New York ($5,000). In 1967 he marries Elsa Astete Millan, a long-time girl friend from his childhood. Harvard University assignes him a post as poetry teacher (1967-68). In 1968 he is nominated member of the Academy of Arts and Science in the States. He publishes "Nueva Antologia Personal" and "El libro de los seres imaginarios".

He starts travelling, giving lectures in different countries and continues his incessant writing through dictation. He lectures in Tel Aviv and the States, publishes "El elogio de la sombra" and "El informe de Brodie" (Doctor Brodies' report) and many others.

Among the countries he visits are: Brasil, Mexico, Israel, Iceland, Scotland, Spain, and Italy. In 1970 he divorces his wife. That same year he is awarded the $25,000 International Inter-American Prize of Literature of Sao Paulo State (Brasil). From Israel he gets the Jerusalem Prize for $2,000.

In 1971 Oxford University nominates him Doctor Honoris Causa. In 1972 he publishes "El oro de los tigres" and in 1973 he retires from the National Library in Buenos Aires. He travels to Mexico where he is awarded the Alfonso Reyes Prize. In the following years, almost until his death, he travels, lectures and publishes extensively. Maria Kodama, his secretary and companion over the last ten years, accompanies him. He will visit Chile, the States, Italy, Geneva, Egypt, Japan, France, Canada, Puerto Rico, Mexico, Sicily, Morocco, Lisbon and Greece. He publishes "Obras Completas" "El Congreso" "La rosa profunda" and "El libro de arena".

In 1976 after the death of Peron and when the Peronist government is overtaken by the military, he endorses their action and is much criticized in the cultural circles of Europe. He visits General Videla (Head of the Junta) together with Ernesto Sabato and other writers to investigate the "disappearance" of Argentinian intellectuals. That same year the Swedish academic Artur Ludkvist declares that for political reasons, Borges will never receive the Nobel Prize of Literature.

In 1977 the University of La Sorbonne nominates him Doctor Honoris Causa. With M.E. Vasquez he stars a collection: "La biblioteca di Babele" of fantastic literature for F.M. Ricci of Milan (about 30 volumes). During the next years he publishes: "La moneda de Hierro" "Que es el budismo" with Alicia Jurado; "Historia de la noche" (poems) "Rosa y Azul", "La cifra", "Nueve ensayos dantescos" and "Los conjurados". He is awarded during those years: The Great Prize from the Spanish Royal Academy

(5 million pesetas). In Paris the Prize Cino Del Duca (200,000 francs). Sandro Pertini, president of Italy gives him the Balzan Prize in 1981 ($140,000). Mexico gives him the Ollin Yoliztli Prize ($70,000). In France, President Mitterrand gives him the Legion of Honour. In the States he receives the Foundation Ingersoll Prize ($15,000). Sicily gives him the "Golden Rose" as a homage to wisdom. Italian editor F.M. Ricci presents him 84 golden sterling for each of his years of life. In 1985 he goes to Italy and then to the States where a ballet on one of his stories is staged. He stays in Geneva until the end of the year. His health deteriorates. The book "Borges en dialogo" is published in Buenos Aires (series of dialogues with Osvaldo Ferrari). The 22 of April of 1986 he marries Maria Kodama. They both leave Buenos Aires and settle in Geneva where he dies the 14th of June 1986.

Despite his confesed agnosticism, before he died he asked and received spiritual assistance from Father Pierre Jaquet, a Catholic Swiss priest. The Swiss government paid him an official hommage, and following his instructions he is buried in Saint George's cemetery in Geneva.

BORGES

BUENOS AIRES, 1985

This interview with Borges, if it could be called that, is singularly un-Borgian. It is not "literary" but full of amiable feelings. It is almost a personal souvenir; like a casual chat under the trees.

It didn't happen in a garden but in the writer's apartment in downtown Buenos Aires. Nonetheless, that is the impression it gives me and which I want to share, as someone who shows a photograph of a particularly pleasant moment in life.

It is a Sunday in June 1985 and Osvaldo Ferrari has arranged a meeting with Borges for this morning.

Osvaldo and I have known one another for 10 years. We have shared a lot in those years, some in Toronto and Montreal, where he also lived for some time.

Among the surprises of this re-encounter, he presents me with a book entitled: "Borges in Dialogue", which is a compilation of conversations between Borges and himself. The first edition of the book sold out very quickly in Argentina (1985).

My first remembrances of Borges stem from the time when as a student at the National Film Institute, a documentary was made on his life and works. And a few years later I met up with him again, during the making of "Borges para millones" a feature film for the European market in which I worked as a Production assistant. Meanwhile there was a continuity before, during and after these encounters. I was simply one of the thousands of "porteños", "who saw Borges walking with his cane through the streets of Buenos Aires".

The writer leaves this afternoon for the States, where he has been invited to give a series of talks. It is part of the innumerable engagments and trips he takes all over the world. A world that pays him honour and respect, and with just reason.

Nominated for the Nobel Prize of Literature several times, every year admirers and colleagues are disappointed that he never receives the prize itself, for Borges has surpassed all expectations in reality.

Winner of the Cervantes Prize – the maximum distinction to which a Spanish–speaking writer can aspire, to name just the most recent – Jorge Luis Borges is considered today as one of the most important contemporary writers. He is a classic.

At 11 a.m. I arrived at the Maipu street apartment. The windows are ajar, the shutters slightly open and one can still hear the street buzzing below.

Borges is standing in the middle of the living–room in an impeccable grey suit. Osvaldo does the necessary introductions. My natural inhibitions are immediately dispelled by the writer's cordiality and friendly manner.

He starts by telling a curious anecdote about a relative of mine, Manuel Galvez (Argentinian novelist) and his loyalty towards him, when Borges was Director of the National Library. His posture and attitude, as of a constant interrogation, belie the blindness and the fact he will be 86 years old in August. He is in an excellent mood and while interchanging stories about Canada – where he has been several times – he suddenly remembers the epic of the Indian Chief Pontiac in North America.

He asks Osvaldo to read him part of that history to refresh his memory. We sit on the sofa below the window and while Osvaldo reads, Borges comments. He laughs, asks, and is amazed. I am too, but more by Borges than by Pontiac.

* * * * *

Borges: When I was in Texas in 1961, I was told the Comanches and the Texan Indians, were better riders than the cowboys. The gauchos were excellent too, but overall the Indian was always a better horseman.

Ferrari: "In 1662 an Indian prophet among the Delawares preached a union of the Indians to expel the English ..."

Galvez: Delaware. Now that has become a street in Toronto. Last names are transformed into streets (laughs).

Borges: (laughs) Yes. The destiny of a lot of Argentinians is to become a street or a railway station. Peron's destiny now. There will be a time, when we will not know if he is a street near Bartolome Mitre (Argentinian President) which is another street near Sarmiento (Argentinian President); which is a street... That's why Lugones (Argentinian poet) forbade his name to be used as a placename. But, even against the complaints of his family, there is a street called Lugones poet. And there is another one in Villa Urquiza, named after his grandfather, Colonel Lugones...

Galvez: It is as if they lose something.

Borges: Yes. It's a form of transmigration. Persons transmigrate and convert into places.

Ferrari: "and in that year, as in 1761, there were abortive conspiracies to massacre the English garrisons of Detroit, Fort Niagara and Fort Pitt, now Pittsburgh..." -where you are going now...

Borges: Pittsburgh yes, that's true, where I'm going now.

Ferrari: "Pontiac, seemed to have been chief of a magic association the Metay, and he took advantage of the religious fervour and general unrest among the Indians to organize, in the winter of 1762, a simultaneous attack on the English forces to be made in May 1763, at a certain phase of the moon...

Borges: (To Ferrari as he stands up) Would you please lead me to the washroom? How strange that preoccupation with the moon...isn't it? (They come back a few minutes later) It is very beautiful all this...

Ferrari: "On the 27 of April 1763, before a meeting near Detroit of delegates from most of the Algonquin tribes, he outlined his plans..."

Borges: You see? Yes. It means he was a man of genius, because for a red skin to organize all that... They were probably very elemental people. Well, the Aztecs were conquered by a handful of "Gallegos" (Spaniards) (laughs). Peru fell as well...and they were thousands; of course the other side had fire guns and horses, sure.

Galvez: Borges, if it's all right with you, I'm taping this... I think all the references to Canada are interesting.

Borges: Yes, of course.

Ferrari: "...on the 20th of May, reinforcements from Fort Niagara were ambuscated near the mouth of the Detroit. In June, the Wyindot and the Potowatomi withdrew from the siege, but the 25th of July they attacked reinforcements. 280 men, including 20 of Rogers Rangers from Fort Niagara, under Captain James Darsel, who however gained the fort in spite of Gladwin's opposition, on the 31st of July attacked Pontiac's camp but was ambuscated at Bloody Run and was killed".

Borges: Of course, there were very few people. Probably hundreds, but not thousands. And not too many hundreds either...

Galvez: Yes. 280 it seems.

Borges: Yes, but that was nothing, a mere skirmish, but of great consequence, naturally.

Ferrari: "...nearly 60 others were killed or wounded. On the 12th of October, the Potowatomi, Ohiwa and Wyandott made peace with the English, while the Ottawa Pontiac continued the siege until the 30th of October when he learned from Neyon de Villiers, commander of Fort Chartres among the Illinois, that he would not be aided by the French. Pontiac then withdrew to the Maumee. Fort Pitt, with a garrison of 330 men, under Captain Simeon Ecuyer was attacked on the 22nd of June, and was besieged from the 27th of July to the 1st of August when the Indians withdrew to meet a rally expedition of 500 men, mostly Highlanders under Colonel Henry Bouquet, who had set out from Carlisle, Pennsylvania.

Borges: Yes, what is the United States now... Pennsylvania.

Ferrari; "...and the 2nd of August, but was surprised on the 5th and 6th and fought the battle of Bushy Run. 35 men south east of Fort Pitt, finally flanking and routing the Indians after treating them by a feinted retreat of a part of his force. Bouquet reached Fort Pitt on the 10th of August. At Michilimackinac, Michigan, on the 4th of June, the Indians gained admission to the Fort by a trick; killed nearly a score of the garrison and captured the remainder, including Captain George Heatherington the commander, besides several English traders, including Alexander Henry. Some of the captives were seized by the Ottawa, who had taken no part on the attack. A part of these were later released and reached Montreal on the 30th of August. Seven of the prisoners kept by the Ojibwa, were killed in cold blood by one of their Chiefs. Fort Sandusky, on the side of Sandusky, Ohio, was taken on the 16th of May by the Wyandot, and Fort St. Joseph, on the site of the present Niles, Michigan, was captured on the 25th of May and eleven men out of his garrison of fourteen, were massacred. The others were taken to Detroit and exchanged for Indian prisoners. On the 27th of May, Fort Miami, on the site of Fort Wayne, Indiana, surrender to the Indians, after his commander in St. Holmes, had been treacherously outsly killed"...

Borges: Yes, treacherously... well, you see, Indiana, Pennsylvania. Canada, naturally...all these facts have been forgotten by now, haven't they?

Ferrari: But there was a line of forts like here, during Alsina's (Minister of War of President Julio A. Roca) time....

Borges: Yes, but the Indians attacked. Pontiac must have been an extraordinary man. Of course, and now... well, it's the name of a car. (laughs).

Galvez: That changed from "Pontiac" to "Pontiac".

Borges: Yes, the Miami were a tribe from the north...

Galvez: I've just remembered the meaning of the Indian word Toronto. It's not "This is the place" but "meeting place".

Borges: Ah yes, yes...meeting place.

Ferrari: "...and with his men, Bradstreet returned to Oswego in November, having accomplished little of value. An expedition of 1,500 men under Coronel Bouquet, left Carlisle, Pennsylvania, in August, and near the site of the present Tuscarawas, Ohio, induced the Indians to release their prisoners and to stop fighting. That was the practical end of the conspiracy. Pontiac himself made submission to Sir William Johnson on the 25th of July 1766 at Oswega, New York. In April 1796, he was murdered when drunk, at Cahokia, nearly opposite St. Louis, by a Kaskakia Indian, bribed by an English trader. And he was buried near St. Louis Fort. His death occasioned a bitter war in which a remnent of the Illinois was practically annihilated at Starvet Rock, between the present Ottawa and Lasalle, Illinois, by the Potawatomi who had been followers of Pontiac.
Pontiac was one of the most remarkable men of the Indian race in American history; and was notable in particular for his power of organization, rare among the Indians."

Borges: It seems that's how he was, yes.

Galvez: Nevertheless, one associates the Canadian Indians with rivers and canoes, instead of horses, like here...

Borges: Yes. But, we don't know...possibly voyageurs, hunters, woodcutters yes. Let's see what Francis says. I have this book, that I read as a boy, after reading Prescott's Conquest of Peru. I think he was from New England. Francis Parkman...How does it start?

Ferrari: Parkman Francis (1823-93) member of a prominent Boston family...

Borges: Ah...you see, Boston! New England. It seems that everybody was from New England. Canada has produced little and New England has produced...well, almost everything; Emerson, Emily Dickinson, Thoreau, Hawthorne...Poe, who was born in Boston, yes.

Ferrari: "graduated from Harvard 1844..."

Borges: Harvard, Cambridge, Massachusetts...yes.

Ferrari: "... having already indicated his interest in frontier life, through excursions to the northern heights to study Indians. After a European trip, 1843–4, he attended Harvard Law School, although he never applied for admission to the Bar. In 1846 he set out from St. Louis on a journey to Wyoming, with the dual purpose of studying Indian life and improving his fragile health."

Borges: Wyoming of course, there he could indeed study the life of the Indians.

Ferrari: "He observed frontiersmen and Indians at first hand, and gained valuable information, but his strenuous exercises led to a complete breakdown. Incapable of writing, he dictated to his cousin and companion, Quincey A. Shaw, his account of the journey, which she entitled "The Oregon Trail" (1849). Parkman continued to suffer from a complete exhaustion and derangment of his nervous system, a mental condition prohibiting concentration, and extreme weakness of the eyes. He was frequently unable to compose more than six lines a day".

Borges: Nevertheless he wrote that much. I don't even attain that... well maybe six lines a day, depending on the day or book.

Ferrari: "He had to hire others to read and write for him..." No friends! (laughs) "...and employed a special instrument enabling him to write without looking at his manuscript. Nevertheless in 1848, he began his "History of the Conspiracy of Pontiac" (1851).

Borges: What date? A year before Caseros (famous battle in Argentinian history). Well, it doesn't matter that much.

Ferrari: "The first of a long series of histories of the French and English struggle for colonial America".

Borges: (To Galvez) Well, we've learned something. So when you go back to Canada, you could get a book on the epic of Pontiac, very easily.

Galvez: I would also like to take some of your memories back with me, including this tape...

Borges: By all means. I don't have any books of mine at home.

Galvez: Really? Why not?

Borges: No, nor books about me. Except for an inoffensive version... (laughs)... for the archives...

Galvez: You say that you don't re-read your work...why not?

Borges: No. I think it's sickening; one must think of the future. In my case, the future could end today. I am 85 years old... but if I commit the imprudence of living longer... I'll be 86 in August. My mother reached 99, with the fear of arriving at 100 years old. In the mornings she would be in an absolute state, because she hadn't died during the night. Until one night, about ten years ago, she didn't wake up. She kept her lucidity until the very last months...

Galvez: Your mother was a woman who was very dear to everyone in Buenos Aires. She was greatly respected...

Borges: Very vital, yes. We discovered America, in the year 1961, when I went to the University of Austin, Texas, to deliver a paper on Argentinian Literature. I am an honorary citizen of Austin and Texas. (laughs) Which is strange for an Argentinian citizen, don't you think? A lot of Spaniards attended. There was a Galician Nationalist, Martinez Lopez, who wanted Galicia to become part of Portugal, because he hated the Castillians and thought that Galicia and Portugal were one, and that a spirit of union between them, was absurd.

Galvez: As you said before, perhaps Canada has produced very little up to now, but there is a feeling...

Borges: Yes, but as Kipling used to say: "How strange, on one side of an arbitrary border line, you have ethics, justice, order and tranquility, while on the other there is crime and disorder..." Crime and disorder were the United States, of course. But the United States has produced many geniouses, while Canada to date, has been singularly arid...

Ferrari: Canada represented order.

Borges: Of course.

Galvez: It's a contradiction in terms. In the same way as happened here. Argentina is a country that doesn't function well in the social sense, but it produces exceptional individuals...

Borges: Perhaps it is more important to function as a social body. Because I'm not sure if the exceptions...

Galvez: The common good is more important.

Borges: I hope that in Canada... Are there gangsters and Mafia there too?

Galvez: Yes, I guess there are...

Borges: Well, (laughs) of course. And here that's almost all there is. Yes, that's true. Have you lived a long time in Canada?

Galvez: Almost 6 years. I haven't left Toronto...

Borges: I know it fairly well, but not the North. It's so cold up there. Trees and bears...that have their coats...(laughs). And the interminable snow, yes. But Alaska must be worse. The territory that borders the United States and Russia. Canadians look towards the States, I suppose...

Galvez: Yes. That surprised me when I arrived.

Borges: Well, yes, because the United States is one of the great powers and Canada is the Lady of the Snows...

Galvez: Toronto being so English, W.A.S.P. even though it isn't anymore. It was the British stronghold.

Borges: Oh yes. White, Anglosaxon, Protestant...yes.

Galvez: In the last ten years there have been big changes. The Portuguese arrived, the Chinese, Italians, Greeks...

Ferrari: ...and Levesque... (laughs)

Galvez: There is an enormous immigration.

Borges: Did you say Greeks? Are there Greeks there?

Galvez: Yes, I believe the Greek community is the third in importance...

Borges: But where?

Galvez: In Toronto.

Borges: I didn't know that...

Galvez: Yes. There're the Italians, the Portuguese, the Greeks...

Borges: Italians well... Portuguese too? But Greeks, that is very strange...So there is a Greek colony?

Galvez: Yes, and a very large one. I talked to many Greeks in the streets, in restaurants, and one of them, a shoemaker, who had lived in Toronto for 25 years, told me that Greece today is a country of woman and children. The men have had to leave...

Borges: How strange... A Greek shoemaker in Toronto! I was in Greece many times. They are very nationalistic. The Turkish style coffee is called "Helenicos". They don't like the Turkish very much, yet they have a lot of Turkish blood, of course.

Ferrari: There's also a lot of English immigration to Canada.

Galvez: Oh yes, as well as Scottish and Irish.

Borges: Oh really? What do they work as?

Galvez: Well, earlier on lots of them worked in construction, stone, masonry...

Borges: Oh yes, masons...

Galvez: ...they were constructors who worked marvellously well; you can see proof of their work today...

Borges: What is the population in Toronto?

Galvez: Around 3 million...

Borges: I didn't know it was that big. When I was in Canada I went to Ottawa, Montreal, Quebec, Toronto. I believe Leacock, Stephen Leacock the humourist was Canadian, wasn't he?

Galvez: Yes he was.

Borges: And there is a poet, Pratt...who has a poem ...a salute to Canada, yes. He has an "Ode to the Railroad"... a railway poet...doesn't augur well (laughs)...but, why not? Everything can be a theme for poetry. Kipling wrote to "Our Lady of the Snows", Canada. Our lady of the snows, yes. And with the enormous territory they have...

Galvez: And almost the same population as Argentina.

Borges: But they are mostly in the south, aren't they?

Galvez: Yes. The majority lives along the border with the States.

Borges: And further away...forests, snow and very raw winters. The winter is very hard in Canada. Well, it's even intolerable deep south, in New Orleans. It was so cold we couldn't go out, for our faces would hurt. We used to walk in Michigan when it was -20 C and it was quite normal. You didn't even speak about -10 C. It was like 20 here, you wouldn't comment on that.

Galvez: Yes. And in Canada once you've gone below 25, it doesn't matter anymore; it's the same...

Borges: Of course, it's because the thermometer is much more sensitive than the human being. They use the Farenheit system there, don't they?

Galvez: Yes and no. They've used both Celsius and Farenheit. Now they've changed to Celsius.

Borges: The Imperial system is absurd...

Galvez: Arbitrary in many ways.

Borges: 12 pennies to a shilling and 20 shillings to a pound... and a guinne is 21 shillings, yes. And the crowns, florins and half crowns... Spencer wrote a defence of that system. I don't know what kind of argument he could find.

Galvez: The English can be very arbitrary. I recall my father – who used to play tennis often – saying: "Why do the English have to count the points in 15's? 15 to 0, 30 to 0. 45 to 0... (laughs) and not 1, 2, 3 and game, which is much practical."

Borges: I didn't know that. That's in tennis? I don't know anything about tennis. Well, it's because they are individualists and traditionalists at the same time. England is very strange. Their moneytary system was absurd... with the florin and half crowns...

Galvez: ...and the pounds.

Borges: Pennies. I believe there is a Norwegian coin called the penie. That's almost the same word. And Fenig in German. Fenig and penny are the same word. Fenig would mean cent while the pennies...

Ferrari: Nevertheless, the English proved they had great financial talents. (laughs).

Borges: It's true. Having to work with those impossible numbers...

Galvez: Exotic perhaps...

Borges: Well, the Americans learned... yes. Now, what are dimes... is that ten cents?

Galvez: Yes, a dime is ten cents. A quarter, 25 cents.

Borges: Yes. They say box... also bones...

Galvez: Sometimes they say nickel too.

Borges: What is a nickel?

Galvez: Nickel is five cents.

Borges: Five cents, I believe here too. Well, five cents that doesn't exist anymore. I remember that until 1930 a shaving was 20 cents and 10 for the tip... yes. (laugh).

Galvez: A big tip! Almost desproportionate to what it is now, that is ten per cent of the bill.

Borges: True. Well, a little cup of coffee would cost 15 cents and 5 cents the tip. Then you had the streetcars for labourers at 5 cents. And all the 10 cents streetcars, which were much more comfortable than the bus...

Ferrari: Well, maybe now we're going back...

Borges: So it seems.

Galvez: And now with the Australes (new Argentine currency) we're going back to the cents.

Borges: We have as a matter of fact, yes. I remember when I was a little boy, the dollar was worth 2 pesos and 50 cents.

Galvez: In what year was that?

Borges: Around 1910, 1914. And the pound sterling, not the notes, but the coins, with the King or the Queen face on them, and with St. George killing his dragon on the other side. That gold coin was worth the same as the Argentinian, but that had the Liberty figure; a 20 cent coin, the Liberty head with the "gorro frigio" (phrygian cap) yes, it was worth twelve pesos and fifty cents. As I was a child, I preferred to collect pounds sterling. I liked the idea of St. George and the dragon... because the Liberty was a coin of 10 cents. And I collected pound sterling that cost me twelve and fifty cents. I had a piggy bank with pounds sterling and now... they have disappeared, as it has in England too. The golden coin has disappeared. There were pound notes, not pounds. Everything was very cheap in Buenos Aires. My father bought the six volumes of Gibbon's "Decline and Fall of the Roman Empire". hand-bound and it cost him six pesos... (smiles).

Galvez: Six pesos, how incredible!

Borges: He bought a house, in the shores of the Rio de la Plata, in Palermo. It was a house with two patios, a garden, a dining-room, vestibule, servant's room a grapevine in the second patio, a terrace... you name it. And all that cost him 13.000 pesos in 1897, to be paid in thirteen monthly payments. But of course Palermo, was a new neighbourhood; the street wasn't even cobbled; it was a dirt track and besides it was a doubtful neighbourhood, near the Maldonado area, in the back of the woods...

Galvez: Yes, that was a very special era.

Borges: We had a summer house in Adrogue "la Rosalinda", that had to be sold later, on Macias street, near the Adrogue's old hotel...

Galvez: That was the time when people came to Argentina to "make it in America". My dentist who lives in Acassuso used to tell me...

Borges: Oh yes, Acassuso. I don't know that neighbourhood well, I know the other side better: Banfield, Lomas, Temperley...

Galvez: ... that his father came from Spain, I believe, to work in the railways. I don't recall the year but it was at the beginning of the century...

Borges: Yes, Talleres and Remedios de Escalada (railway stations) were made. That was the time of the railway workers.

Galvez: He said his father, by working on the railways had bought for each of his seven sons, a house as a present. By his work, he was able to give each of his sons a house!

Ferrari: Seems incredible...

Borges: Yes. They used to sell the land plus 1.000 bricks, I remember well how my father, who went blind and was an English literature professor in "Lenguas Vivas" (Living Languages) earned 100 pesos. But he also had another salary, a good one, as Secretary in the Law Courts. Now, for people who had retired, it was cheaper to live in Europe; the Argentine peso was strong. So much so that in Geneva there were a lot of Argentinians, Chileans and Venezuelan pensioners, who received their income there. The Argentinian peso was stronger than the Swiss-Franc and it was less expensive to live in Europe than in Buenos Aires. And much nicer too, because to live in Geneva is lovely, yes. (laughs) Isn't strange? There were also a lot of Uruguayans, because the Uruguayan currency was also strong. And now... I don't know, we are the last card of the deck...

Galvez: Yes... we've slipped back to the 45th place I believe, terrible...

Borges: Yes. How terrible. And well... We will climb back, if we don't keep slipping down. (laughs) We shouldn't despair.

Galvez: We'll get back, yes. I'm optimistic about it.

Borges: Oh yes, me too. We must have faith. We have the duty of faith. Although everything seems so difficult now. The Government is so mediocre. But in any case, we suppose they are gentlemen, don't we?

Galvez: Yes...

Borges: Not gangsters... we suppose.

Galvez: Supposedly.

Borges: We also suppose that about the military, yes. (laughs)

Galvez: Or at least, there is an intention of being so.

Borges: That's what I believe. In any case the alternative to this Government is dreadful. So we should back them, I believe.

Galvez: Yes, because I think that there isn't even an alternative...

Borges: Beyond Pacho O'Donnell (Argentinian playwriter and Secretary of Culture) and all those things like... "The seduction of the superintendent's daughter", that is worse than the title. The seduction of the superintendent's daughter... what a title! Who could think of such a thing? Well, it seems those are the kind of books that sell.

Galvez: But one notices – I noticed it after such a long absence from Buenos Aires – after witnessing this change in the currency for example, that the people want to make this change, work. There is a will and faith for the better.

Borges: Oh yes... of course, naturally. Because if things don't work for the better, this will be chaos.

Galvez: Exactly.

Borges: The alternative is terrible of course. In this moment... we should all be Radicals (Party that won the last elections) (laughs). (To Ferrari) Should I put my coat on then...?

Galvez: Thank you very much, Borges.

Borges: No, thank you.

Osvaldo helped him on with his coat. It was a bit late and the three of us walked to the door.

While waiting for the elevator, the conversation continued uninterrupted until we said goodbye downstairs, at the main entrance.

In that brief journey, Borges had time to ask questions, to compare Argentina and Canada, to talk about the masks, totems and Canadian Indians. His memory, precision, irony and innocent spirit were intact and more than amazing. I felt sorry I could not stay on for hours and hours. We said goodbye and set off in different directions.

Back in Canada again, I tried to co-ordinate with Greg Gatenby and Osvaldo Ferrari, Borges' presence at the Toronto Harbourfront International Authors Festival. (1985) There were talks too, of some Canadian Universities who would have paid him honours. Borges, despite his busy schedule, was very happy with the idea of the trip. But soon after that, he was sick and the visit didn't take place. Several months later I received the news of his death. It happened in Geneva: the place where he had once been happy. Being 86 years old, he didn't want "to commit the imprudence of living for too long" and so it was granted to him.

I cherish a last image: one of Borges carrying his cane, with Osvaldo walking away down Maipu Street. I find it difficult to think, as surely many people in Buenos Aires will, that Borges will not walk those streets anymore.

PRINCIPAL WORKS BY JORGE LUIS BORGES:

(Original title, year of first edition and publishing house. Unless otherwise noted, all originated in Buenos Aires, Argentina.)

"Fervor de Buenos Aires" (1923, Imprenta Serantes)
"Luna de enfrente" (1925), Proa)
"Inquisiciones" (1925, Proa)
"El tamaño de mi esperanza" (1926, Proa)
"El idioma de los Argentinos" (1928, Gleizer)
"Cuaderno San Martin" (1929, Proa)
"Evaristo Carriego" (1930, Gleizer; 1955 Emece)
"Discusion" (1932, Gleizer; 1957, Emece)
"Historia universal de la infamia" (1935, Tor; 1954, Emece)
"Historia de la eternidad" (1936, Viau y Zona: 1953, Emece)
"Antologia Clasica de la Literatura Argentina" (1937, Kapeluzt) (In
        collaboration with Pedro Henriquez Ureña)
"Pierre Menard, autor de Don Quijote" (1938)
"Antologia de la Literatura Fantastica" (1940, Sudamericana) (Collaboration with
Adolfo Bioy Casares and Silvina Ocampo)
"El jardin de los senderos que se bifurcan" (1941, Sur)
"Antologia poetica Argentina" (1941, Sudamericana) (Collaboration with
        Bioy Casares and Silvina Ocampo)
"Seis problemas para Don Isidro Parodi" (1942, Sur) (With A. Bioy Casares
        under the pseudonym of H. Bustos Domecq)
"Poemas" (1943, Losada) (Poem collection 1922–1943)
"Los mejores cuentos policiales" (1943, Emece) (In collaboration with
A. Bioy Casares)
"Ficciones" (1944, Sur; 1956, Emece)
"El compadrito" (1945, Emece; 1968, Fabril) (Anthology of Argentinian
authors in collaboration with Silvina Bullrich)
"Un modelo para la muerte" and "Dos fantasias memorables" (1946, Oportet &
        Haereses) (With A. Bioy Casares)
"Nueva refutacion del tiempo" (1947, Oportet & Haereses)
"El Aleph" (1949, 1952, Losada; 1957, Emece)
"Aspectos de la Literatura Gauchesca" (1950, Numero, Montevideo, Uruguay)
"La muerte y la brujula" (1951, Emece)
"Antiguas Literaturas Germanicas" (1951, Fondo de Cultura Economica,
        Mexico City) (With Delia Ingenieros)
"Los mejores cuentos policiales, segunda serie" (1951, Emece) (With
        A. Bioy Casares. Sequel to the previous one.)
"El lenguaje de Buenos Aires" (1952, Emece) (With Jose A. Clemente)
"Otras inquisiciones" (1952, Sur; 1960, Emece)
"El Martin Fierro" (1953, Columba) (With Margarita Guerrero)
"Los orilleros" and "El paraiso de los creyentes" (1955, Losada) (Two
        screenplays with A. Bioy Casares)
"Cuentos breves y extraordinarios" (1955, Losada, 1967, Rueda) (Anthology
        with A. Bioy Casares)

"La hermana de Eloisa" (1955, Ene) (With Luisa Mercedes Levinson)

"Leopoldo Lugones" (1955, Troquel) (With Betina Edelberg)

"Manual de Zoologia Fantastica" (1957, Fondo de Cultura Economica, Mexico
        City) (Collaboration with Margarita Guerrero)

"El Hacedor" (1960, Emece)

"Libro del cielo y del infierno" (1960, Sur) (Anthology with A. Bioy
        Casares)

"Macedonio Fernandez" (1961, Culturales Argentina)

"Antologia personal" (1961, Sur)

"Literaturas Germanicas Medievales" and "Introduccion a la Literatura
        Inglesa" (1965, Falbo; 1965, Columba) (Both in collaboration with
        Maria Esther Vasquez)

"Obra poetica" (1964, Emece) (Poetic works 1923-1964)

"Introduccion a la Literatura Norteamericana" (1967, Columba) (With Esther
        Zemborain)

"Cronicas de Bustos Domecq" (1967, Losada) (With A. Bioy Casares)

"Para las seis cuerdas" and "El otro, el mismo" (1967, Emece)

"Nueva antologia personal" (1968, Emece)

"El libro de los seres imaginarios" (1967, Kier; Fondo de Cultura
        Economica, Mexico City, 1967)

"El elogio de la sombra" (1969, Emece)

"El informe de Brodie" (1970, Emece)

"El Congreso" (1971)

"El oro de los tigres" (1972, Emece)

"Obras completas" (1974, Emece)

"La rosa profunda" (1975, Emece)

"El libro de arena" (1975, Emece)

"La biblioteca di Babele" (1975, F.M. Ricci, Milan, Italy) (Collaboration
        with Maria Esther Vasquez. 30 volumes)

"Prologos" (1975, Torres Aguero Editor)

"La moneda de hierro" and "Que es el Budismo" (1976, Emece) (With Alicia
        Jurado)

"Libro de suenos" (1976, Torres Aguero)

"Historia de la noche" (1977)

"Nuevas Cronicas de Bustos Domecq" (1977, La Ciudad)

"Rosa y Azul" (1977, Sedmay, Madrid, Spain)

"Obras completas en colaboracion" (1979)

"La Cifra" (1981, Alianza Editorial, Madrid, Spain; Emece 1981/81)

"Borges el memorioso: conversaciones con A. Carrizo" (1982, Fondo de
        Cultura Economica, Mexico City)

"Nueve Ensayos Dantescos" (1982, 2nd Edition, Editorial Espasa-Calpe
        1983)

"Atlas" (1985, Translated by A. Kerrigan, New York: Dutton 1985) (Photos
        by Maria Kodama)

"Los conjurados" (1985, Alianza Tres, Madrid, Spain)

"Borges en dialogo" (1985, Grijalbo) (Collection of dialogues with Osvaldo
        Ferrari)

"Libro de dialogos" (1986, Sudamericana) (Collection of dialogues with
        Osvaldo Ferrari)

BIBLIOGRAPHY ABOUT BORGES

ENGLISH TRANSLATIONS

The Aleph and Other Stories 1933-1969. Translated by Norman Thomas di Giovanni
in collaboration with the author. New York: Bantam Books, 1970.

The Book of Imaginary Beings. Margarita Guerrero, coauthor. Translated by
Norman Thomas di Giovanni in collaboration with the author. New
York: Avon Books, 1970.

The Book of Sand. Translated by Norman Thomas di Giovanni. New York: E.P.
Dutton, 1976.

Chronicles of Bustos Domecq. Adolfo Bioy Casares, coauthor. Translated by
Norman Thomas di Giovanni. New York: E.P. Dutton, 1976.

Doctor Brodie's Report. Translated by Norman Thomas di Giovanni in collabora
tion with the author. New York: E.P. Dutton, 1972.

Dreamtigers. Translated by Mildred Boyer and Harold Moreland. Austin:
University of Texas Press, 1964.

Ficciones. Edited by Anthony Kerrigan, with various translators. New York: Grove
Press, 1962.

Labyrinths. Edited by James Irby and Donald Yates. New York: New Directions,
1962.

Other Inquisitions. Translated by Ruth L.C. Simms. New York: Washington
Square Press, 1966.

Works Dealing with Borges

Alazraki, Jaime. *Jorge Luis Borges.* New York: Columbia University Press,
1969.

--. "Kabbalistic Traits in Borges's Narrations." *Studies in Short Fiction*
8, no. 1 (Winter 1971): 78-92.

--. *La prosa narrativa de Jorge Luis Borges.* Madrid: Gredos, 1971.

Anderson-Imbert, Enrique. "Un cuento de Borges: 'La casa de Asterion.'" in
Jorge Luis Borges, edited by Jaime Alazraki, Madrid: Taurus, 1976.

--. "Nueva contribucion al estudio de las fuentes de Jorge Luis Borges."
Filologia (Buenos Aires) 8 (1962): 7-13.

Barnatan, Marcos. Jorge Luis Borges. Madrid: Ediciones Jucar, 1972.

Barrenechea, Ana Maria. La expresion de la irrealidad en la obra de Jorge Luis Borges. Mexico: El Colegio de Mexico, 1957.

--. Borges: The Labyrinth Maker. Translated by Robert Lima. New York: New York University Press, 1965.

Barth, John. "The Literature of Exhaustion." The Atlantic Monthly 220, no 2 (August 1967): 29-34.

Becco, Horacio Jorge. Jorge Luis Borges: Bibliografia total, 1923-1973.

(Buenos Aires: Casa Pardo, 1973.)

Berg, Mary Guyer. "The Non-Realistic Short Stories of Lugones, Quiroga, and Borges." Ph.d. dissertation, Harvard University, 1969.

Borges. [No editor listed]. Buenos Aires: Editorial El Mangrullo, 1976.

Bosco, Maria Angelica. Borges y los otros. Buenos Aires: Fabril Editores, 1967.

Botsford, Keith. "About Borges and not about Borges." Kenyon Review 26 (Autumn 1964): 723-37.

Briggs, John. "Interview with Borges." University Review (January 1970):12.

Burgin, Richard. Conversations with Jorge Luis Borges. New York: Avon Books, 1970.

Chao, Ramon, and Ramonet, Ignacio. "Entretien avec Jorge Luis Borges." Le Monde 19 April 1978, p.1.

Charbonnier, Georges. El escritor y su obra. Mexico: Siglo Veintiuno Editores, 1967. Spanish translation of Entretien avec Borges. Pares: Gallimard, 1967.

Christ, Ronalk. Interview with Borges. Paris Review 40 (Wintor-Spring   1967): 116-64.

--. The Narrow Act: Borges' Art of Allusion. New York: New York University Press, 1969.

"Desagravio a Borges." Sur 94 (July 1942): 7-34. di Giovanni, Norman Thomas. "Borges's Infamy: A Chronology and a Guide."   Review (Spring 1973): 6-12.

--. Hapern, Daniel; and MacShane, Frank, eds. Borges on Writing. New York: E.P. Dutton, 1973.

Dunham, Lowell and Ivash, Ivar, eds. The Cardinal Points of Borges. Norman: University of Oklahoma Press, 1971.

Fernandez Moreno, Cesar. "Interview with Borges." Encounter 32 (April   1969):
     6–12.

Gallagher, D,P. "Jorge Luis Borges." In Modern Latin *American Literature*, pp.94–
     121. New York: Oxford University Press, 1973.

Gass, W.H. "Imaginary Borges." *The New York Review of Books* 20 Novermber
     1969, pp.5–9

Genette, Gerard. "L'utopie litteraire." In *Figures I*, pp.123–32. Paris: Editions
     du Seuil, 1966.

Gilio, Maria Esther. Interview with Borges. In *Borges*, pp.13–27. Buenos   Aires:
     Editorial El Mangrullo, 1967.

Guibert, Rita. Interview with Borges. In *Seven Voices*, pp.75–117. New   York:
     Random House, 1973.

Gutierrez Girardot, Rafael. *Jorge Luis Borges: Ensayo de interpretacion.*
     Madrid: Editorial Insula, 1959.

Harss, Luis and Dohman, Barvara. "Jorge Luis Borges, or the Consolation by
     Philosophy." In *Into the Mainstream*, pp. 102–36. New York: Harper
     & Row, 1967.

L'Herne (biennial French magazine). *Jorge Luis Borges*. Paris, 1964.

Ibarra, Nestor. *Borges et Borges.* Paris: L'Herne, 1969.

Irby, James. "Encuentro con Borges." *Revista Universidad Nacional de Mexico*
     16, no. 10 (June 1962): 4–10.

––. "Introduction." In *Labyrinths*, edited by James Irby and Donald Yates,
     pp. xv–vviii. New York: New Directions, 1962

––. "The Structure of the Stories of Jorge Luis Borges." Ph.D. dissertation,
     University of Michigan, 1962.

Jurado, Alicia. *Genio y figura de Borges*. Buenos Aires: Editorial Universitaria
     de Buenos Aires, 1964.

Kovacs, Katherine Singer. "Borges on the Right." *New Boston Review* (Fall
     1977): 22–23.

Lida, Raimundo. "Notas a Borges." In *Letras hispanicas*, pp. 280–83. Mexico:
     El Colegio de Mexico. 1958.

Marx, R., and Simon, J. "Interview with Jorge Luis Borges." *Commonweal* 89
     (25 October 1968): 107–10.

Matamoro, Blas. *Borges o el juego trascendente.* Buenos Aires: Editorial A. Pena Lillo, 1971.

Modern Fiction Studies 19, no. 3 (Autumn 1973). Special issue on Borges.

Murillo, Luis. *The Cyclical Night: Irony in James Joyce and Jorge Luis Borges.* Cambridge, Mass.: Harvard University Press, 1968.

La Nacion (Buenos Aires). Interview with Borges (27 April 1976).

Naipaul, V.S. "Comprehending Borges." *The New York Review of Books* 19 October 1972, pp. 3–5.

La Opinion (Buenos Aires). Interview with Borges (15 September 1974).

––. Interview with Borges (9 May 1967).

Prieto. Adolfo. *Borges y la nueva generacion.* Buenos Aires: Letras Universitarias, 1954.

Prose for Borges. [No editor listed]. Evanston, Illinois: Northwestern University Press, 1972.

Rest, Jaime. *El laberinto del universo: Borges y el pensamiento nominalista.* Buenos Aires: Ediciones Libreria Fausto. 1976.

Review. Spring 1973. Special issue dealing with *Universal History of ... Infamy.*

Rodman, Selden. Interview with Borges. In Tongues of Fallen angel, pp.5–37. New York: New Directions, 1974.

Rodriguez Monegal, Emir. *Borges: hacia una lectura poetica.* Madrid: Guadarrama, 1976.

––. *Borges par lui-meme.* Paris: Editions du Seuil, 1970.

––. *Jorge Luis Borges: A Literary Biography.* New York: E.Pdutton, 1978.

––. *El juicio de los parricidas: La nueva generacion y sus maestros.* Buenos Aires: Deucalion, 1956.

––. "Borges, Lector Britannicae." *Review* (Spring 1973): 33–38.

Santana, Lazaro. :La vida y la brujula" (interview with Borges). *Insula* 22, no.259 (May 1968): 1–5.

Sorrentino, Fernando. *Siete conversaciones con Jorge Luis Borges.* Buenos Aires: Editorial Casa Pardo. 1973.

Stabb, Martin S. *Jorge Luis Borges.* New York: Twayne publishers, 1970.

Steiner, George. "Tigers in the Mirror." *The New Yorker*, 20 June 1970. pp.109-19.

Sturrock, John. *Paper Tigers: The Ideal Fictions of Jorge Luis Borges*. New York; Oxford University Press, 1977.

Tamayo, Marcial, and Ruiz-Diaz, Adolfo. *Borges: enigma y clave*. Buenos aires: Editorial Nuestro Tiempo, 1955.

Todo Borges y.... Buenos aires: Editorial Atlantida and *Gente* magazine, n.d.

Vazquez, Maria Esther. Borges. Caracas: Editorial Monte Avila, 1977.

--. "La pasion literaria." Conversation with Borges and Raimundo Lida. In *La Nacion*, 13 February 1977.

Wheelock, Carter. *The Mythmaker: A Study of Motif and Symbol in the Short Stories of Jorge Luis Borges.* Austin: University of Texas Press, 1969.

Yates, Donald. "Behind 'Borges and I.'" *Modern Fiction Studies* 19, no.3   (Autumn 1973): 317-24.

II. INTERVIEWS WITH BORGES

Alcorta, 1964
Alcorta, Gloria: "Entretiens avec Gloria Alcorta," in *L'Herne,* Paris, 1964, pp. 404-408.

Arias, 1971
Arias Usandivaras, Raquel: "Encuentro con Borges," in *Imagen* (no.90), Caracas, February 1-14, 1971, pp.2-5.

Burgin, 1969
Burgin, Richard: *Conversations with Jorge Luis Borges.* New York, Holt, Rinehart and Winston, 1969.

Christ, 1967
Christ, Ronald: "The Art of Fiction XXXIX," in *Paris Review* (no 40), Paris, Winter-Spring 1967,pp. 116-164.

Correa, 1966
Correa, Maria Angelica: An unpublished interview with Borges. Buenos Aires, September-October 1966.

De Milleret, 1967
De Milleret, Jean: *Entretiens avec Jorge Luis Borges.* Paris, Pierre Belfond, 1967.

Fernandez, 1967
Fernandez Moreno, Cesar:"Harto de los laberintos," in *Mundo Nuevo* (no. 18), Paris, December 1967, pp. 8–29.

Guibert, 1968
Guibert, Rita: "Jorge Luis Borges," in *Life en Español* (vol.31, no.5), New York, March 11, 1968, pp.48–60.

Guibert, 1968
Gujibert, Riat: "Jorge Luis Borges," in *Seven Voices.* New York, Knopf, 1973, pp.77–117.

Irby, 1962
Irby, James E.: "Entrevista con Borges," in *Revista de la Universidad de Mexico* (vol.16, no.10), Mexico City, Hybe 1962, pp.4–10.

Latitud, 1945
"De la alta ambicion en el arte," in *Latitud* (no.1), Buenos Aires, February 1945, p.4.

Marx and Simon, 1968
Marx, Patricia, and Simon, John: "An Interview," in *Commonweal* (vol.84, no.4), New York. October 25, 1968, pp. 107–110.

Murat, 1964
Murat, Napoleon: "Entretiens avec Napoleon Murat," in *L'Herne*, Paris, 1964, pp.371–387.

Opinion, 1977
"Las paradojas de Borges contra el castellano y contra si mismo," in *La Opinion*, Buenos Aires, May 15, 1977, p.28.

Peralta, 1964
Peralta, Carlos: "L'electricite des mots," in *L'Herne*, Paris, 1964, pp.409–413.

Plata, 1945
"De novelas y novelistas habla Jorge L. Borges," in *El Plata*, Montevideo. October 31, 1945.

Ribeiro, 1970
Ribeiro, Leo Gilson: "Sou premiado, existo." in *Veja* (no.103), Rio de Janeiro, August 26, 1970,pp.3–6.

Simon, 1971
Simon, Herbert: ''*Primera Plana* va mas lejos con Herbert Simon y Jorge Luis Borges," in *Primera Plana* (no.414), Buenos Aires, January 5, 1971, pp.42–45.

Triunfo, 1969
"Habla Jorge Luis Borges," in *Triunfo* (vol.24, no.389), Madrid, November 15, 1969, pp.35–36.

Vazquez, 1977
Vazquez, Maria Esther: *Borges: Imagenes, Memorias, Dialogos.* Caracas, Monte Avila, 1977.

CRITICAL AND BIOGRAPHICAL WORKS

Alen, 1975
Alen Lescano, Luis C.: *La Argentina ilusionada, 1922–1930.* Buenos aires, Editorial Astrea, 1975.

Anzieu, 1971
Anzieu, Didier: "Le corps et le code dans led contes de J.L. Borges," in Nouvelle Revue de Psychoanalyse, Paris, July–August 1971, pp. 177–210.

Baudelaire, 1951
Baudelaire, Charles: *Oeuvres completes.* Paris, Gallimard, 1951.

Bianco, 1964
Bianco, Jose: "Des souvenirs," in *L'Herne*, Paris, 1964, pp.33–43.

Bioy, 1940
Bioy Casares, Adolfo: "Prologo" to *Antologia de la literatura fantastica.* Edited in collaboration with Jorge Luis Borges and Silvina Ocampo. Buenos Aires, Editorial Sudamericana, 1940.

Bioy, 1942
Bioy Casares, Adolfo: "Los libros," a review of Borges' *El jardin de los senderos que se bifurcan,* in Sur (no.92), Buenos Aires, May 1942, pp.60–65.

Bioy, 1964
Bioy Casares, Adolfo: *La otra aventura.* Buenos Aires, Editorial Galerna, 1964.

Bioy, 1975
Bioy Casares, Adolfo:"Chronology," in *Review 75* (no.15), New York, Fall 1975, pp.35–39.

Borges, 1921
Borges, Jorge (Guillermo): *El caudillo.* Palma (Majorca), 1921. Privately printed.

Britannica, 1911
"The Tichborne Claimant," in *The Encyclopaedia Britannica*. Eleventh edition. New York, Encyclopaedia Britannica Company, 1911. Vol.26, pp.932–933.

Chesterton, 1940
Chesterton, G.K.: *The End of the Armistice*. London, Sheed & Ward, 1940.

Christ, 1969
Christ, Ronald: *The Narrow Act: Borges' Art of Allusion*. New York, New York University Press, 1969.

Clouard, 1947
Clouard, Henri: *Histoire de la litterature francaise: du symbolisme a nos jours (de 1885 a 1914)*. Paris, Albin Michel, 1947.

Corominas, 1967
Corominas, Joan: *Breve diccionario etimologico de la lengua castellana*. Madrid, Gredos, 1967.

Cozarinsky, 1974
Cozarinsky, Edgardo: *Borges y el cine*. Buenos Aires, editorial Sur, 1974.

De Gourmont, 1912
De Gourmont, Remy: *Promenades litteraires*. Quatrieme serie. Paris, Mercure de France, 1912.

De Quincey, 1897
De Quincey, Thomas: *Collected Writings*. Edited by David Masson. London, A.C. Black, 1897. Vol.3.

De Torre, 1925
De Torre, Guillermo: *Literaturas europeas de vanguardia*. Madrid, Caro Raggio, 1925.

De Torre, 1965
De Torre, Guillermo: *Historia de las literaturas europeas de vanguardia*. Madrid, Aguilar, 1965.

Fernandez, 1967
Fernandez Moreno, Cesar: *La realidad y los papeles*. Madrid, Aguilar, 1967.

Genette, 1964
Genette, Gerard:"La litterature selon Borges," in L'Herne, Paris, 1964, pp.323–327.

Gobello, 1953
Gobello, Jose: *Lunfardia*. Buenos Aires, Argos, 1953.

Grondona, 1957
Grondona, Adela: *El Grito Sagrado (30 dias en la carcel)*. Buenos Aires, 1957. Privately printed.

Ibarra, 1964
Ibarra, Nestor: "Borges et Borges," in *L'Herne*, Paris, 1964, pp.417–465.

Ibarra, 1969
Ibarra, Nestor: *Borges et Borges*. Paris, L'Herne editeur, 1969. A revised and enlarged version of the 1964 article.

Irby, 1971
Irby, James E.: "Borges and the Idea of Utopia," in *Books Abroad* (vol. 45, no.3), Norman (Oklahoma), Summer 1971, pp. 411–419.

Jurado, 1964
Jurado, Alicia: *Genio y figura de Jorge Luis Borges*. Buenos Aires, Editorial Universitaria, 1964.

Klein, 1975
Klein, Melanie: *Love, Guilt, and Reparation and Other Works*. New York, Delta, 1975.

Lacan, 1966
Lacan, Jacques: "Le state de miroir comme formateur de la fonction de Je," in *Ecrits*. Paris, Editions de Seuil, 1966, pp.93–100.

Levine, 1973
Levine, Suzanne Jill: "A Universal Tradition: The Fictional Biography," in *Review 73* (no.8), New York, Spring 1973, pp.24–28.

Lucio and Revello, 1961
Lucio, Nodier, and Revello, Lydia: "Contribucion a la bibliografia de Jorge Luis Borges," in *Bibliografia Argentina de Artes y Letras* (nos.10–11), Buenos Aires, April–September 1961, pp. 43–112.

Marechal, 1948
Marechal, Leopoldo: *Adan Buenosayres*. Buenos Aires, Editorial Sudamericana, 1948.

Marechal, 1968
Marechal, Leopoldo: "Claves de Adan Buenosayres," in *Cuaderno de navegacion*. Buenos Aires, Editorial Sudamericana, 1968, p. 133.

Megafono, 1933
"Discusion sobre Jorge Luis Borges," in *Megafono* (no. 11), Buenos Aires, August 1933, pp.13–33.

Moore, 1929
Moore, Thomas: *The Poetical Works*. Edited by A.D. Godley. Oxford, Clarendon Press, 1929.

Mother, 1964
Acevedo de Borges, Leonor: "Propos," in *L'Herne*, Paris, 1964, pp.9–11.

Neruda, 1974
Rodrigues–Monegal, Emir: "[Neruda:] The Biographical Background," in *Review 74* (no. 11), New York, Spring 1974, pp.6–14.

Ocampo, 1961
Ocampo, Victoria: "Saludo a Borges," in *Sur* (no. 272), Buenos Aires, September–October 1961, pp.76–79.

Ocampo, 1964
Ocampo, Victoria: "Vision de Jorge Luis Borges," In *L''Herne*, Paris, 1964, pp. 19–25.

Ocampo, Silvina, 1964
Ocampo, Silvina: "Image de Borges," in *L'Herne*, Paris, 1964, pp.26–30.

PEN, 1937
PEN Club de Buenos Aires: *XIV Congreso Internacional de los PEN Clubs.* Buenos Aires, 1937.

Petit de Murat, 1944
Petit de Murat, Ulyses: "Jorge Luis Borges y la revolucion literaria de Martin Fierro," in Correo Literario, Buenos aires, January 15, 1944, p.6.

Pezzoni, 1952
Kinzie, Mary, ed.: "Prose for Borges," in *Tri–Quarterly* (no. 25), Evanston (Illinois), Fall 1972.

Reyes, 1943
Reyes, Alfonso;"El argentino Jorge Luis Borges," in *Tiempo*, Mexico City, July 30, 1943, p.104.

Rivera, 1976
Rivera, Jorge B.: "Los Juegos de un timido," in *Crisis* (no.38), Buenos Aires, May–June 1976, p.23.

Rodriguez–Monegal, 1970
Rodriguesz–Monegal, Emir: *Borges par Lui meme.* Paris, Editons de Seuil, 1970.

Sanguinetti, 1970
Sanguinette, Horacio S.: *La democracia ficta, 1930–1938.* Buenos aires, Editorial Astrea, 1975.

Videla, 1963
Vignale, Pedro Juan and Tiempo, Cesar, eds.: *Exposicion de la actual poesia argentina 1922–1927*. Buenos Aires, Editorial Minerva, 1927.

Yates, 1973
Yates, Donald A.: "Behind 'Borges and I,'" in *Modern Fiction Studies* (vol.19, no.3), West Lafayette (Indiana), Autumn 1973, pp.317–324.

Zigrosser, 1957
Zigrosser, Carl: *The Expressionists*. London, Thames and Hudson, 1957.

MARCO DENEVI

*H*e was born 12 May, 1922 in Saenz Peña, a suburb of Buenos Aires. He lived in the same house until 1980, when he moved to the neighbourhood of Belgrano, closer to down-town Buenos Aires.

Son of Valerio Denevi, a Genovese indus-trialist who prospered in Argentina, and Maria Eu-genia Buschiazzo, he is the youngest of seven broth-ers and sisters.

He went to Law Uni-versity, but after five years with only one term to go, he found it bored him. So he disrupted his career and started writing a novel, which he had been thinking about for several years. The novel "Rosaura a las Diez" published in 1955, got the First Prize in a contest sponsored by Editorial Kraft and has been a best seller in Argentina ever since.

A play, "Los Expedientes", written in a week, was staged by the National Comedy in the Cervantes Theatre and won a National Prize for the comedic genre. It was published in 1957. It is used at the Universities of Michigan and Indiana as a test for their Spanish Literature classes. That same year he adapted his novel "Rosaura a las Diez" for the screen in collaboration with film Director Mario Sofficci. The film won the National Film Institute's First Prize and the Critic's Award in Argentina.

In 1958 he travelled to Europe as part of the Argentine representatives at the Cannes Film Festival. "Rosaura a las Diez" was nominated for best plot at that Festival.

In 1960 he won Life Magazine's First Prize for Latinameri-can writers, with a short novel "Ceremonia Secreta". He also staged "El Emperador de la China" in the Teatro Comico of Buenos Aires. The play was published the same year.

In 1961 he adapted "Ceremonia Secreta" for television. The production won the Argentinian TV's top Prize "The Martin Fierro".

He decided not to compete anymore in any literary constest in Argentina. In that way he remained to this day voluntarily out of any National or Provincial literary competition.

In 1962 he opened the play "El Cuarto de la Noche" (The Room of the Night) in the Candilejas Theatre. It won the Argentinian Writers Guild Prize. Convinced that he had not what it took to write for the theatre, he destroyed all the copies of the work.

In 1966 "Falsificaciones" (an apocryphal anthology) appeared and also the novel "Un pequeño cafe".

In 1968 he abandoned the job he had for the last 15 years as Jefe de la Asesoria Letrada de la Caja Nacional de Ahorro Postal (Chief of the Legal Advisory Office of the Argentine Postal Saving Bank). From then on he dedicated himself to writing. That same year the film adaptation of "Secret Ceremony" was shot in England, directed by Joseph Losey (Elizabeth Taylor, Mia Farrow, Robert Mitchum). The original novel had already appeared in several editions in the States (in Spanish and in English) and in Argentina.

In 1970 he published "El Emperador de la China y otros cuentos" and also "Parque de Diversiones" (various genres).

In 1972 the novel "Los asesinos de los dias de fiesta" was launched and in 1973 a collection of short stories "Hierba del cielo" followed. The Editorial Universitaria de Santiago de Chile published his "Antologia precoz".

In 1974 and 1975 respectively he published "Salon de Lectura" and "Los Locos y los Cuerdos" (short stories). In 1977 "Reunion de Desaparecidos" (short stories). In 1978 he wrote a series for television "Division Homicidios" and won the Argentores Prize again.

In 1979 "Parque de Diversiones II" appeared in a revised and enlarged edition and in 1980 he wrote "Robotobor" stories for children.

In 1981 he was given the Esteban Echeverria Prize by Gente de Letras as a tribute for all his works. He started contributing to the Buenos Aires newspaper "La Nacion". His political articles, some of them extremely polemical always attract a wide readership.

In 1982 he published "Araminta o el Poder" (various genres). His contributions to the newspaper "La Nacion" earned him several awards, among them: Cruz de la Universidad John F. Kennedy, Cruz de Plata Esquiu, Gran Premio Anual de la Liga Argentina Pro Comportamiento Humano. He confessed once his indebtedness to the English writer Wilkie Collins (1824-1889) who is considered to be one of the finest detective story writers of all time.

In 1983, Editorial Celtia of Buenos Aires published "Paginas de Marco Denevi seleccionadas por el autor", a selection of his own best writing.

In 1985 he published the novel "Manuel de Historia".

Marco Denevi still lives in Belgrano in Buenos Aires. He is a member of the Argentinian Academy of Literature and continues to contribute to several national newspapers.

DENEVI
BUENOS AIRES, 1985

In the cultural spheres of Buenos Aires, there are very few people who don't know Fanny Ezcurra's name. Through her past and present apartments, many of the artists and intellectuals who have given Argentina prestige, have met, become friends, quarrelled, made-up and above all, enjoyed themselves.

As a putative son, something we have agreed on as long as I can remember, I have certain rights and privileges. One of them allowed me to do this interview with Marco Denevi in her house.

Marco was always there at those "cultural nights" in Fanny's place during my teens. They were full of music, discussions, guitars, readings, wine and empanadas. They are filled with memories of Hernan, Federico Nunez, Pepe, Marta Lynch, Juan, Teresita and so many others. We called him Marco, because for us he was only Denevi outside Fanny's house. And Marco was already Marco Denevi of course. That man, some 20 years older than us, whose "remise" (rented limousine) would wait - sometimes until 2 or 3 in the morning - to take him back to his home in Saenz Peña. He was the writer of "Rosaura a las Diez" ("Rosaura at ten O'clock") and "Ceremonia secreta" ("Secret ceremony") and probably one of the best contemporary Argentinian writers. This didn't escape us. But being adolescents, at least I, felt a certain pride, mixing shyness with some arrogance, that prevented me from open admiration. Something that I hope to correct now.

Tonight at Fanny's apartment, there are also empanadas and wine. Seven years have passed since the last time we saw one another. It seems no more than a few days. And so the conversation starts up. Everybody has changed little. Well, that's an understatement. Instead of being a teenager I'm now 39 years old. Marco has greying temples. These are the envy of those wishing for the "distinguished look". He rejects the idea saying that time passes not in vain. We don't agree in his case.

Marco chain smokes. I didn't remember he smoked so much. But it is a peculiar way of smoking. Two or three puffs and then he puts it out. A few minutes later he lights another and the ceremony (not very secret) repeats itself. The result is an ashtray that starts looking like an exotic paperweight. Full of mysterious white and grey worms.

Marco is eloquent and precise, sometimes edgy as a knife while at others nostalgic in the most casual way. He talks, get excited as if thinking aloud; sails in and out of humour, erudition – with no desire to impress – and everyday language. This is a difficult combination that in his case comes together spontaneously. It's also one of the literary traits in his novels and short stories. There are so many now they are compiled in various volumes. He has achieved, among many other things, a death blow to solemnity, a typical Argentinian evil. He has done it, hopefully for ever, without falling into vulgarity and with a deep knowledge of the language. Using it, as a good surgeon uses a scalpel, almost without effort.

Many times he has said he would have liked to be a film director. He'd probably be an excellent one. It's enough to go over the precision of the images and ideas in any of his stories. It seems they are pinned to an imaginary screen. And most surely because of that original expressive strength, two of his novels have been made into films.

The first "Rosaura at ten o'clock" was made by Mario Sofficci, one of the best Argentinian Directors. The second, "Secret Ceremony" was directed by Joseph Losey, one of the best English Directors, starring Elizabeth Taylor, Mia Farrow and Robert Mitchum.

His career, diverse and prolific as few others, started 30 years ago with the Kraft Prize in Buenos Aires for his novel "Rosaura at ten o'clock".

In 1960 he won the Life Magazine Prize for Latinamerican writers with "Secret Ceremony". Northamerican readers are acquainted with the English version of that work. Then recently, Canadians have heard of it through Alberto Manguel's adaptation for CBC radio (Toronto).

Several essays on his fiction have been published in the States, among them "Myth in the work of Marco Denevi", University of Maryland (1977). "The kaleidoscopic reality in the work of Marco Denevi" by Ivonne Revel Grove.

A Passionate lover of music, opera, theatre and films, he has worked on different genres from novel and short stories to aphorisms, poetry and journalism. His last novel "Manuel de Historia" ("Manuel of History") has just appeared in Buenos Aires to excellent reviews.

He has written short story collections such as "The Emperor of China" (1970) "Grass from heaven" (1973) "Reading salon" (1974) "The crazy and the sane" (1975) "Reunion of the dissapeared" (1978) and many others. Throughout his work, Marco Denevi has an obsession, an obsession he senses deeply, which is to give ethical sense and a voice to the marginals of History. Those people who make up the vast majority of our world.

* * * * *

Galvez: Marco, how did this writing adventure start?

Denevi: In a very casual way, you see literature wasn't my forte. I'm lucky really, for I have several. Music is one of them.

Galvez: Really? I didn't know.

Denevi: Yes, I would give all my writing to be able to compose one piece that satisfied me.

Galvez: Do you play as well as compose?

Denevi: Well, a long time ago when I had a piano, I played tangos and composed some pieces. I did the soundtrack for the TV play "Secret Ceremony"... but like Chaplin I hid my name. Such modesty!

Galvez: Did you use a pseudonym?

Denevi: No, there was no author attributed to the piece, but I wrote it. I became a writer because I knew how to read and write. It was the only thing left out. So at the age of 32, I had an idea for a piece. I wrote it in about 2 months. It became a novel and the novel won a prize. In that way, from one day to the next I became a writer, without knowing I was one.

Galvez: The novel was "Rosaura at ten", which won the Kraft Prize, in 1955. Was that when your career began?

Denevi: It was the first thing I wrote. It was as if someone had pushed me in front of an audience, so that I could act. But I didn't know the play nor what to do. So it took me five years to convince myself I was a writer.

Galvez: So in 1957 you wrote a play for the theatre.

Denevi: Well, isn't really a work I should speak of. The fact that I always loved theatre so much made me fall into the trap of thinking I could write it!
I wrote "Los Expedientes" (The Dossiers/Records) in a week. Augusto Mario Delfino, a friend, took it to the Director of the Argentinian National Comedy, and one day I was reading the theatre program in the newspaper, and there it was. But I hadn't done anything. I still think the play is very bad. So bad that it alone convinced me, my love for the theatre was a non-requited love. I never tried again.

Galvez: But you did another one...

Denevi: Yes. But as a reading piece not to be played. The fact that an incredible audacious irresponsible person, staged it, is his business.

Galvez: In 1960 you wrote "Secret Ceremony".

Denevi: That's right. It was a short novel - a novella in fact - that had the good fortune of winning...

Galvez: Well, I wouldn't call it good fortune because...

Denevi: No, no Raul...

Galvez: ...there were more than 3.000 entries for the LIFE Magazine Latin american Writer's Awards. So that's not just good luck, is it?

Denevi: Yes it is luck. One should never be proud of winning an award, most of all in those conditions. One of the jury members, Hernan Diaz Arrieta, a Chilean, publically announced that when he got the entries - about 1.000 in all, that had previously been selected by a reading committee - he was terrified. So he began reading, and the first work he laid his hands on, was a story that flowed well and interested him. So he chose it for the award. If I had felt any vanity, it was immediately dispelled by what he had to say. He awarded the prize, because the book didn't bore him. Now, who knows how many better works than mine were not even read by him?

Galvez: What happened to "Secret Ceremony" after the prize?

Denevi: Along with the other prize-winning stories in the competition, two editions were published in the States - one Spanish, one English.
Some years later, International Pictures optioned it to produce a film. It was shot in London, England, directed by Joseph Losey, with Liz Taylor, Mia Farrow and Robert Mitchum.

Galvez: How did you feel about the film version of your work?

Denevi: I am totally indifferent to the translation of literary works into screenplays. To the contrary, I think a director or screenwriter, should be able to think the story over from square one.
That's to say they must think of the same story but in another language. It shouldn't be a mechanical transposition from book to film. I don't care that the story was adapted when transposed. I am more worried when the screenplay doesn't satisfy me, especially in the second half of the film. You know what I mean, when the tension lags and the audience is left wandering... what's this all about?
I have to admit I didn't like the film. I went to see it, not to check if it was a good or bad adaptation of my book. The first part of the film, and the relationship between the characters played by Liz taylor and Mia Farrow is very good. Then a third character is introduced. It's a man, who was played by Robert Mitchum. That's when the story becomes absurd and incomprehensible.

Galvez: Which is not the case in your book.

Denevi: Not at all. The appearance of the male in my story is very brief, but at the same time meaningful and very important. It's only a scene, that explains what happened before, and gives meaning to what's going to happen later on.

Galvez: Yes, that is a frequent filmic mistake. The adaptors try to be faithful to the book not realizing it is another language and therefore needs another interpretation.

Denevi: Of course. It is another genre. What did Shakespeare do with Bandello's story? He made Romeo and Juliet! And who would even question whether Shakespeare was faithful or unfaithful to the original? He did something else! And he did so well, that it naturally erased everything that was created before. Take operas for example. There are magnificent operas based on theatrical pieces.

Nobody expects the opera to be a sound or singable adaptation of the theatrical piece. What you expect is that the opera will be good.
There are enormous differences between Verdi's Othello, with script from Boito, and Shakespeare's Othello. But they are both masterpieces, and you couldn't ask for anything more.

Galvez: What happened after "Secret Ceremony"? You wrote a novel. Then those plays – to be read as you said – and afterwards you have written short stories.

Denevi: Yes...I think as a consequence of my resounding failure in theatre, I returned more ardently to literature, touching different genres, the novel for example. I wrote two more and now I just handed the fourth, over to the publisher.

Galvez: Is this one the last novel?

Denevi: Yes. I wrote short stories. I wrote brief plays "to be read". I wrote little pieces – a bit like glossaries – called "Falsifications". I did aphorisms, newspaper articles... I tried to exhaust all the genres, as a kind of revenge.

Galvez: And poetry?

Denevi: Lately I've written some poems. I'm not sure yet if they are poetry or versified prose. I don't know if they're meant for poetry of for recitals.

Galvez: What is the title of this last novel?

Denevi: It's called "Manuel de Historia". It has been twelve years since my last novel. I've changed so much in twelve years... The world changes, reality changes. So this novel is very different from the previous ones. It has another tone, structure and technique.
Many readers will say: but this is not Denevi... Of course they are thinking of Denevi from twelve years ago. There's little of him today in me. Don't they say that we completely change all our cells and tissues, every seven years? It's been twelve years. It means I'm almost two times removed from who I was, when I wrote the last novel.

Galvez: In your short stories and novels, there is a preference for certain weak characters, loners or marginals. Why?

Denevi: Because I totally agree with Marcel Schowb when he says that History pays attention to generalizations and the great movements, taking into account the individual only in relation to these collective movements. Meanwhile it olympically disregards the individual adventure, individual characteristics and only emphasizes social undertakings, which he calls historical. Literature rescues individual adventure. What would we know about the individual if it wasn't for literature? Neither science nor history say much about it. Schowb says literature will tell us that this man had one eye bigger than the other; that another wore a certain kind of cloth, while yet another had particular sorrows and anguishes.

Man doesn't live history "generally speaking". Generally speaking man suffers history, he is not the main character in history.

Galvez: Someone tells him later?

Denevi: Someone tells him... Heredoto said cuttingly: Historic facts happen always, while the man in the street is somewhere else, in another time. He never feels like the protagonist of historical facts. History speaks of the masses or about the great leaders; Alexander The Great's speeches and Napoleon are not those of the common man. Common man's history is literature work. That's why the psychoanalists have to resort to literature. It is there they find the description, analysis and the search for what human nature is in the individual sphere. And it is that, that is so rich.

The writer will always have material to work with, for individuals are unique. All Kings, are in a way the same character. It is the individual, with his changes, that provides the material with which the writer can work.

Galvez: About the characters and your creation... Is it true - as the saying goes - that every novel is autobiographical?

Denevi: No. Not that I want to become the universal legistator of all writers... But I believe every writer is an individual, so I don't see why what he says about himself should be valid for the rest.

The view point is the only harshly autobiographical element in my work. I can only look at the world from my own interior perspective. But in general, my characters are a montage of real people. None of them are exact replicas. But they combine features that exist in reality. That's what nature does when it combines features of several human beings into someone who is the result of all of them. My characters are the ones I found, the ones I know and try to rescue from the anonymity history would condemn them to. But only my perspective is autobiographical and the vision I have of them. In that sense I remember Nieztche's saying in "Human too Human": "The writer has to give his word to the experience and the passion of the other".

Galvez: In this case, your profession has to do with that?

Denevi: Yes. I've been dedicated full-time to literature for 16 years. I feel a little bit like a historian. But while the historian makes history of the history, I make history of the unhistorical: the ones who couldn't make it into history. From there on, I give the word to characters who in real life are silent, humble, marginal.

Galvez: They have someone to talk about them...

Denevi: Exactly. And that's why I'm not interested in the ones who have a voice and a vote. I'm interested in the ones who don't have either, so that in literature they'll have both.

Galvez: Maybe this is due to your being a lawyer.

Denevi: Maybe...

Galvez: Do you write because you are impelled to?

Denevi: Well, I don't make a sublimation of my profession as a writer. The idea of the writer dying to write is not for me. Perhaps I would die if I was obliged to write...(laughs) In that case, yes. I write because by now, I don't know how to do anything else. So I do what I know and try to do it as best as I can. If there are a lot of people who don't like it, I'm not to blame. I try my best. The right man in the right place is perhaps the synthesis of all this. I think that the function I have in society, overall in Argentinian society, is to write.

Galvez: You're also a musician. Do you see a connection between literature and music?

Denevi: Perhaps so, because I feel for the euphony of words. A cacophony in prose makes me jump. If I'm not a musician it is because I don't have the technique; it's too late to learn it. Being a musician requires an entire life and well... I have to console myself with the role of the listener. In regards to music it is not bad to be the enjoyer of music written by others.

So I'm a great listener, a great Opera spectator. That is a beautiful role too.

Galvez: And at the same time, I guess that gives you the good rhythmic sense that belongs as much to literature as it does to music.

Denevi: Yes, literature has that sense of interior rhythm. Even in prose there's an interior rhythm that a fine ear can detect and enjoy. Without disregarding what moral values are associated to music. For example in The Merchant of Venice, Shakespeare says that a man insensitive to music, is a man made for treason and whose feelings are black as the night... It's surprising, isn't it? I believe a man insensitive to music is a man insensitive to the Universe for its nature after all, is sonorous.

Galvez: Ingmar Bergman used to say he constructed his films musically.

Denevi: Yes, that's how it is. The truth is that all this goes back to Plato and the Orphics. Cervantes also says that where is music there's no evil. He gives music a moral value.
Shakespeare in Julius Caesar, speaking of Brutus, says that Brutus has a fault that worries him for he doesn't like music. Why doesn't he say poetry or painting? He mentions only music. And he counts it as a moral fault. And I agree with that.
A 17th century man meets fifteen people a day. In the 20th century he meets thousands. In that sense our experience is vast. And I've arrived at this conclusion: a man deaf to music is deaf to others. There is a moral or spiritual deafness in people insensitive to music. On the other hand I feel that everyone who is emotionally sensitive to music and are moved to tears by it, are morally good. Shakespeare said it much better and before me.

Galvez: How do you write Marco? Do you have a special time of day and discipline?

Denevi: Well, my discipline comes from my personality, not from my will. I have deliberately not adopted a discipline. My way of being has taken me to a work technique that consists in working every day, without expecting raptures of inspiration. No, no. I write every day. I write definitively to the last draft. I don't make "work-prints".

Galvez: What you've written stays that way?

Denevi: Yes. If I make mistakes, the page goes in to the garbage and I start again. But I have never made drafts. What I write, I write it "sub especil-aeternitatis" if you like. Once and for all.

Galvez: You don't correct afterwards?

Denevi: Afterwards, minor details that doesn't weight in the narration, will be corrected. For example an adjective; "this" for "that" in a page; a full stop transformed into a coma in another; a word scratched on page three...and that's all. But the body of the text stays practically in it's intirety. That makes me write, naturally, with a certain intensity, because I think I can't make mistakes...
If I was to write drafts, I believe I would write any puerility. This doesn't mean I don't do it when I believe I'm writing for eternity, but that's another problem...

Galvez: Mugica Lainez (Argentinian writer) said something similar, I believe. He said that he wrote by hand and that he would correct while typing. There were two processes. When asked why, he would say: "because I have a certain facility and if I didn't, if writing would be such a sacrifice, I wouldn't be a writer".

Denevi: Of course, and the craft is what facilitates things. Isn't it? The craft shortens the time one needs to write. Whatever one was set to write.
When an Argentinian novelist confessed me that all his novels had gone through six or seven different versions, I couldn't believe it. It meant that the novel he had published was written about six times. He transformed it continuously. First he would do a sketch and then develop it. This was modified and so on until he arrived at the final version. That is absolutely incomprehensible to me, because it's not in my character. I have to write the novel directly on a first impulse.

Galvez: And it comes out like that, the whole thing?

Denevi: Oh yes, yes. Now maybe afterwards it's all wrong perhaps... but in the moment I'm writing, it coincides with what I want to write.

Galvez: So you discipline yourself daily into that position...

Denevi: I have become a disciplined, daily writer. As Ravel would say, like a Swiss watchmaker who is in front of his working table every day, mantling and dis-mantling clocks. Quite coldly

I would say, I'm a bit like that. That doesn't mean there aren't moments when it seems someone else is dictating the text. Or others when I have to search for it, agonizing at my desk. Many silences, difficulties with much sweat – I won't add "blood and tears" because it would be an excessive metaphor – and in any case, with a lot of perspiration.
But then, there are moments when the text flies as if I did no more than make it visible.

Galvez: So you have these surprises... when it seems someone else wrote what you're reading?

Denevi: Yes, yes, yes! For instance when it's the time for proof-reading or when it's published a long time after it was written. I read it almost as if it wasn't mine. Sometimes I'm surprised and say – and this is not immodesty – "this is very good!". But it's not immodesty nor vanity because I'm not praising my own work but someone else's work. And I praise the dexterity as I praise it in any other writer.

Galvez: What is a writer then?

Denevi: I don't know. Perhaps the definition would be frightingly simple. The writer is someone who writes and publishes. I remember once, someone asked a singer what a soprano is, and she said "a soprano is someone who has a particular voice pitch". I don't know what a writer is, but if I have to give him an ethic mission beyond the literary, I would say he gives voice to those who don't have it in reality.
I believe the writer's greatest glory is as Longfellow once perceived it. Maybe it's an apocryphal story but it doesn't matter. They say one day Longfellow was walking near the village where he lived, and heard children singing a poem of his with music from a nursery rhyme. He went and asked the children what they were singing, and they replied "we don't know". Longfellow wrote later: "I have arrived at the height of my glory, I am an anonymous poet". (laughs)

Galvez: Your complete works are already on sale, aren't they?

Denevi: Yes, they are printing them... To me this business of "Complete works" sounds premature and necrological at the same time. Don't you agree? (laughs).

Galvez: (laughs) Yes, I was going to ask you about that. How do you feel about it?

Denevi: When they speak of "Complete works", it's like saying "well my friend, you don't have anything else to write, you've written everything you could, don't write anymore". I had suggested to the editor to call them "Incomplete works", but he thought it was a joke in poor taste and didn't accept it. (laughs).

Galvez: Torontonians and Canadian readers in general, probably don't know many Argentinian writers – with the exception of Borges perhaps – which is a pity. Borges is the only one known outside of the country. It would be good for them – and for Argentina – to know many others.
The economic situation in Argentina or maybe the lack of promotion and other circumstances, means they are postponed or left alone.
What do you think about that, and which writers from Argentina and elsewhere do you prefer?

Denevi: First let say that if Borges' figure has eclipsed the rest, it is the others' fault. If we had Borges' genius, perhaps we could fight hand-in-hand with him. Overall Borges has jeopardized – without wanting to or without premeditation – those of us who have a similar education and produce literature in tune with his. So of course people who aren't fools, they prefer the best and disregard the inferior categories. Naturally, between Borges and Denevi, they choose Borges. The reason is very simple: the best of Denevi is even better written by Borges. So then why would they want me?

Galvez: Well...

Denevi: That is one thing. I believe however that there are Argentinian writers who deserve to be better known. Were you thinking of contemporary writers?

Galvez: No, not necessarily, because I think it's a novelty for Canadians to know any Argentinian writers apart from Borges. From 80 years back to the present day.

Denevi: There are great Argentinian writers who are not much read even by Argentinians, but who nevertheless express very original realities. They manage to touch on things, all we writers search for. That original note. That initial opening that great geniuses have.
Benito Lynch for example, is not well known inside or outside of Argentina. Among contemporaries, there is Adolfo Bioy Casares who I admire enormously. I wouldn't say all of his works are

masterpieces, but for a writer I think it is enough to write one. And he has several that deserve universal acclaim.

Bioy Casares wrote a very Argentinian novel, that has an almost metaphysical tone. It's called "El sueño de los heroes" (The Heroes's Dream). Curiously enough, it's not his best-known work not even in Argentina; but it is an absolutely genial and amazing novel. He is also the author of a short novella entitled "La invencion de Morel" (Morel's Invention), that is years ahead of many things done later on. It also proposes a truly admirable theme. Then there is a novel "Los viernes de la eternidad" (The Fridays of Eternity) by Maria Granata, that stands up well against the magical realism of tropical Hispanoamerican literature. It's a beautiful novel, wonderful. With an overpowering flight of the imagination.
I don't know why these works have not gone beyond the country's borders. It is a pity. I believe a non-Argentinian would have a richer, more complete vision of Argentina, through these writers.

Galvez: You mentioned Maria Granata, a woman writer. Do you think there are differences between female and male writers?

Denevi: No, I believe a great writer is epicene...

Galvez: Asexual?

Denevi: No, doubly sexed. When Flaubert is asked who Madame Bovary is, he says "Madame Bovary is me" and it's true. If a writer doesn't know how to identify himself with the female character he deals with, then that female character is false.
Great writers are those who at the moment of writing can be – this has obviously nothing to do with the sexual behaviour of the author, of course – a man and a woman, child and old man. He has to be all the characters and understand them from inside. To identify himself with them and express them authentically.
So a great writer is not man or woman. He is man and woman. When I hear about "feminine literature" I think it must be bad, because if it is good, it is masculine/feminine. As Proust and Stendhal"s literature is. As Truman Capote or Carlson McCullers literature is.

Galvez: If not, you end up doing a special literature for women and another one for men...

Denevi: And that is abominable, don't you agree?

Galvez: Yes, certainly. Do you think there is an Argentinian point of view in literature?

Denevi: In my work?

Galvez: Yes.

Denevi: I believe there is. To start with, I couldn't cease to be Argentinian, even if I wanted to...

Galvez: Bonaerense (from Buenos Aires province), Argentinian or both?

Denevi: Bonaerense perhaps... Not specifically porteño (from Buenos Aires city) because I didn't live in Buenos Aires until four years ago.

Galvez: You were born in Saenz Peña, right?

Denevi: Yes, in the province of Buenos Aires, which is nearby but nonetheless not the capital itself. I was raised in a little town, with all the things that little towns have, but it was not the big city.
Nevertheless, apart from the fact that I can't get away from myself, from the fatality of being Argentinian, I believe that even if I talk about the Minoutaur, Alcistes or Napoleon, you can find Argentinian psychology and characteristics in my literature.

Galvez: Why did you say 'fatality of being Argentinian'?

Denevi: Because being born, raised, educated, growing up and aging in the Argentinian Republic, naturally those cultural, social and political circumstances, have moulded me. Nobody can evade the society he lives in. Henry James became so English... Elliot too, precisely because they lived in England even though none of them were English...

Galvez: Yes, but in a certain way they had, at least Henry James had, a foot on both continents. At the end he felt nostalgia for both worlds...

Denevi: But I don't see that reflected much... perhaps wrong, but that's my point of view. When I read James's work, even when they have American characters – "The Ambassadors" for example – the point of view seems English. His eye is not on the United States side of the Atlantic. It is an eye that judges Northamerica from an European point of view.

Galvez: Yes. But he feels nostalgia about that, doesn't he? It's the other way around; he feels a reverse nostalgia.

Denevi: Yes, it could be also a personal nostalgia, which is understandable. But I don't think his work ceased to be thought, felt, conceived and written from England. The same thing happens to Elliot and so many others, because finally, nationality and birth place are facts that if not accompanied afterwards by one's life development, don't have importance at all.

Galvez: Is it fortuitous you think?

Denevi: Yes, I think is fortuitous. One is born where chance wanted one's mother to be.

Galvez: Two of your novels have been adapted to film: "Secret Ceremony" and "Rosaura at ten". I don't remember which writer said that if he had to decide today, he would probably choose film language. How do you see this alternative?

Denevi: I feel the same. Generally speaking, I think cinema tends to the author's theory, meaning that the Director is the author of the screenplay and everything else. I think cinema strives more and more to break away from literature, because it is a sort of subsidiary that provides it with themes and stories. Cinema tends to give the Director, authorship of the film, as a novelist is the author of the novel. It is the splendid case of Bergman or Fellini. Fellini is sometimes inspired by literature, for example in "Satyricon", but his best films are those in which he is the sole author of the film.
If I were born again – it's not impossible, what is impossible in reality..? – and wanted to be a story teller, I would choose cinema as my language.

Galvez: And today cinematic language has enormous influences on literature, and viceversa. Both seem to feed one another.

Denevi: That's true, because they are like two heirs to the same inheritance. They dispute a domain in which they have many territories. Cinema is closer to literature than to theatre, by all means! Film narrates in another way and with another language, with "visual and sound" images, but it's also a narration.

There is always a story that flows, after all that is the secret and patrimony of narrative.

So there are two ways of telling a story: by the word or by images and sounds, that is film. Confronted with this dilemma today, I would doubtless choose the language of cinema. I would like to be a Director – and as I am speaking of what I would like and not what I could – I would like to be a Director in the style of Visconti, for as far as I'm concerned, he's the great contemporary Director.

Galvez: So I guess you don't like Godard very much. Godard's case is very special. After experimenting with narrative techniques, the jump-cut, and a series of elements he supposedly invented, he's saying now – after 25 years – that stories should be retold.

Denevi: Of course, that happened with literature also. For years literature disengaged itself from what used to be called: the subject and the plot. The word "plot" was almost pejorative. A novel with a plot went out of fashion because it took us back to the Dark Ages. Consequently, thousands of novels were made without a plot. Today, we've relearned, that a story without a plot is not a story. It's not telling us anything. So we go back to the plot.

Among the French directors, Francois Truffaut has always interested me, because of his special mixture of wisdom combined with great spontaneity. You see, I believe the best kind of wisdom is the one that doesn't show itself off.

A film like "La noche americana" (Day for Night) for example, is wonderful. I saw it several times because I enjoyed it like crazy. Truffaut has a way of narrating that is splendid...

Galvez: Did you see a film of his called "Las Dos Inglesas" (Two English Girls) by any chance?

Denevi: Yes...wonderful, beautiful, beautiful... There is another film that I went to see again recently, inspired by a novel – the novel is lovely and the film too – and it's called "El Desierto de los Tartaros" (The Tartar's Desert). A film by Valerio Surlini, with a kind of aseptic quality, cleanliness: with a plastic beauty, beautiful images and first-rate cast: Vittorio Gassman, Max Von Sydow, Giuliano Gemma, Jacques Perrin, Fernado Rey, Paco Rabal... It is almost poetic, it may sound forced but it's a visual metaphor.

It's a long visual metaphor so beautifully expressed, that when people tell me "yes, but nothing happens" I say "well, what happens in a metaphor?"

Galvez: After spending 6 years in Canada and returning to Buenos Aires, it's almost a shock. The other day we were talking about it – and I think you agreed – that there is a corruption of the language. You notice it in the streets, everywhere. What do you think about it? How much literature should improve language?

Denevi: Yes, I think there is corruption, degradation and even prostitution of the language. I wouldn't like to speak of any other country but Argentina. It is serious and it is not an obsession of a linguistic, nor a dictionary reader; not even, as I am, of a member of the Academy.
Speech sets us apart from animals. Man was not a man before he spoke. Man is man, since he speaks. Therefore, any attack on language, is an attack to the human condition. Any degradation of speech it's a degradation of the human condition.
Diderot has a famous anecdote in his book about De Lambert. An apocryphal story perhaps, but nevertheless very revealing. He says that in the King's palace gardens in Versailles, there was a cage with an orang utan inside, who looked almost human. One afternoon, the Cardinal of Pollinac aproached the cage, and observed the monkey for a while. Finding him so close to the human condition he said: "Speak and I will baptize you". Had the monkey spoken, he would have deserved to be baptized; he would have proven he was a man. Of course the monkey didn't speak and proved to be a monkey. So above all, what distinguishes us, as men, is the gift of speech.

Galvez: The Verb.

Denevi: The Verb. Exactly, the Verb. Written language is a very recent cultural invention; it isn't more than 10 or 12 thousands years old. That's nothing really in the history of humanity. But that's not the case for speech. From the moment man, through a gradual process, began to conect the sounds he made with his mental functions; when he could unite voice and thought – which is speaking – we recognize him as a man. That's why language is important. Because it is the 'sine qua non' condition of being a man. So the invention of words means giving each thing a name. Reality is so complex and fluid that one will never understand it. But if one puts names to it, it's established. It can be studied. You can find out it's relations, the bonds that exists between different fragments of that reality. Remember Pascal's remark: "Man is the weakest reed... but it's a thinking reed". And it's because of words one thinks. For you can't think without them. So, if we overcome our essential weakness thanks to the word, why not take care of it?

Galvez: That's true, but then why is it corrupted?

Denevi: Because the word has great power. The word is per se an act of responsability: as the saying goes: "I take the word". To take the word, to take hold of speech, is affirming oneself before others in the face of reality and to become responsible. Irresponsible people have taken the word and prostituted it. You see they take it not to utter it but to misuse it. The word then, allows a series of interpretations that instead of being true, are unreal. The corruption of the word comes through, precisely, from a moral corruption; therefore as language is corrupted, our relation to reality darkens and corrupts too.
We know reality through the names we give it. Everything has a name, and culture is...I would say, the gradual retreat from anonymity. Isn't it?

Galvez: So language is a convention. We *agree* that things are called *this* and not *that.*

Denevi: Yes, and that convention is human... Now the problem starts when the words instead of naming what they've been created for, name other things and deception and confusion arises.

Galvez: And that is very common today, in that a word no longer means one thing; it means fifteen. And we don't even agree on which fifteen, so misunderstandings start...

Denevi: A word means fifteen different things; and then you have the opposite phenomena: fifteen different words name one thing. What is called synonymy. In Argentina the word 'barbaro' means: ignorant, formidable; barbaro means everything! Everything is barbaro. A girl: barbara! A play: barbaro. A person who has comitted a crime is a barbaro. So reality becomes impoverished, because with that synonymy you loose a bit what Azorin called: "la dolencia del matiz" (the pain of degree/shading)...

Galvez: The grey tones...

Denevi: The grey... The grey tones of reality. There is more than one green. And if language doesn't rescue the greens and we call all green, green, we loose the notion of the richness and complexity of reality.

Galvez: Yes, subtlety begins to fade.

Denevi: Yes, you see Raul, that's why there aren't absolute synonyms. The precision of the French or the English language is always being praised. One word means that and not something else. In Spanish there are two words for the same thing. Take for example: "can" and "perro" (dog). They're not exactly the same, there is a shade of difference. We don't call our teeth "perrunos", we call them "caninos" (canine tooth). We don't say John has a "caracter de can"... We say he has a "caracter de perro". (bad temper). "Can" is the aristocratic side of the word "perro" (dog).

Galvez: It's a little bit artificial as well, isn't?

Denevi: Cultural, because as it comes from the Greek it seems that with the word "can" we would like to express the best of the dog; now when we want to put him down a bit we say "perro". So they are not synonyms, we can't use them indeterminately.

Galvez: One doesn't say: I am hungry as a "can"... (I'm starving).

Denevi: No, one doesn't, nor does one day: they brought me a "perruno" (a doggie)... No! They brought me a "canino" che, is my tooth! Isn't it so? (laughs).

Galvez: Exactly... (laughs). Marco, going back to the creative process... As a writer, what paradises and hells you go through?

Denevi: I always remember Borges's definition: "I had thought of paradise as a library..." I don't. I think of paradise as a meadow in which we've all read all the books, and we don't need them anymore. Perhaps we'd dedicate ourselves to music. "The country fete" by Giorgione, is for me a paradisiac image. To make music and sing or as Garcia Marquez says "talk about music", I think that is for me, the image of Paradise. Hell, naturally, would be the contrary. Hell is the absence of Paradise; therefore hell would be the place that isn't a meadow, where nobody has read anything and where's no music...(laughs).

Galvez: What I wanted to ask you, has to do with what we were talking about before: the corruption of lauguage.
People in everyday life in Canada as well as in Argentina make use of a very limited vocabulary. I don't remember the exact number of words, but I believe it is not more than 3.000...

Denevi: Generally it's no more than 1.000...

Galvez: ...and they "get by", so to speak, which is very limiting. Do you think a person who reads, should be therefore educating himself? Should literature widen the use of vocabulary?

Denevi: Yes. I believe literature has to be a bit, the treasurer and manager of language's richness and genuinity.
I think that there is a moral failure in the writer who impoverishes language. I believe he has the moral and social duty, to care for the richness, expressivity and communicatibility of language. To me, writers who are capable of repeating twenty times the same word in a page, seem to impoverish not only language, but also the vision and notion we have of reality. I don't like that. There is, I believe, a moral rather than a literary duty to take care of the language.
The two greatest writers – Shakespeare in English and Cervantes in Spanish literature – were contemporaries and died the same year. Both are the greatest exponents, statistically, of linguistic richness. They both surpass the 15.000 vocables. In the case of Shakespeare reaching I believe 18.000, in a moment when the Englsih language had 60.000 terms, which is a record. I believe that shows a moral quality in them both.
A language that is poor will consequently lead to a bad conception of reality. I don't mean that because I know many words, I'm going to have many ideas. But, how could I have many ideas if I have few words?

Galvez: Which indicates that it is always better to possess an extensive vocabulary, and from there move to the ideas...

Denevi: That's right. You know very well that today the linguistic repertoire of languages has increased enormously.
There's been a lot of interchanges too. Today, between scientific, technical and other terms, there must be more than 400.000 vocables in Spanish.
I'm not saying one should use them all, but neither should I reduce my vocabulary to a thousand and no more.
Reality itself has broadened. What did the men of the XV Century knew of what we know today?
To know more, naturally means amplifying language to start with. Certain things cannot be expressed without new words. I can't talk about electronics, computers, cibernetics or nuclear physics, if it isn't precisely through a new vocabulary created for them.

Galvez: We wouldn't have problems in this case, in taking words from other countries – the States or England for example – and adapting them...

Denevi: Yes, adapt them, why not?

Galvez: ...or take them as they are. I had a surprise in Canada for example, with the word "patio". They will say "the patio", using the Spanish word "patio" with the same meaning, and many others also.

Denevi: Many others of course, because hasn't culture been universalized a bit? Isn't there, as they say, a "unification of field"? So then, that also carries into a unification of language as well. And going to the extreme: shouldn't we strive for the creation of a universal language? Not an artificial one like Esperanto or Volapuk, but one in which all languages spontaneously converge... How well we'd understand each other!

Galvez: Before the Tower of Babel...

Denevi: Yes... exactly. The image, the metaphor of Babel, is revealing. God, to punish men, multiplies languages. The Bible then says: "and for that reason they were dispersed throughout the face of the Earth..." To be reunited again, we should go back to the time before the Tower of Babel.

Galvez: Yes...

Denevi: But in an spontaneous way not artificially.

Galvez: ...yes, because probably Esperanto was part of that intent, as you said. And French or Latin before...

Denevi: And now English.

Galvez: And also now there is an intent to return to the Spanish Empire. So it seems.

Denevi: Yes, because we shouldn't forget that there are more than 300.000.000 human beings, who speak Spanish. It's a vast linguistic domain. I don't think that there are many languages that could dispute the ground with Spanish speakers. But it would be beautiful if in the XXI Century, all men could speak a language formed by the watershed of every language existing today!

I would then travel the world understanding all men, and many human conflicts would dissappear...

Galvez: Yes, it would be wonderful.
When I was leaving for Canada someone told me: "remember that even if you know English or another language, noone arrives at the same intimacy one had in one's own". And it's so true. It doesn't matter how well you know it.

Denevi: Yes, yes. It's true, it's true... Because it is terrible to live in a country, whose language one doesn't understand.
When Ovid was exiled to the Ponto Ausinus – that was on the Black Sea – he writes to a friend: "I feel like a barbarian" (he who was a Latin Poet!) "because I'm surrounded by people who don't know Latin".

PRINCIPAL WORKS BY MARCO DENEVI:

(Original title, year of first edition and publishing house. Unless otherwise noted, all originated in Buenos Aires, Argentina).

"Rosaura a las Diez" (1955, Kraft)
"Los Expedientes" (1957, Talia)
"Ceremonia Secreta" (1960, Calatayud)
"El Emperador de la China" (1970, Libreria Huemul)
"Falsificaciones" (1966, Eudeba)
"Un pequeño cafe" (1966, Calatayud)
"El Emperador de la China y otros cuentos" (1970, Libreria Huemul)
"Parque de Diversiones" (Emece)
"Los asesinos de los dias de fiesta" (1972, Emece)
"Hierba del Cielo" (1973, Corregidor)
"Antologia Precoz" (1973, Editorial Universitaria de Chile)
"Salon de lectura" (1974, Libreria Huemul)
"Los Locos y los Cuerdos" (1975, Libreria Huemul)
"Reunion de Despaarecidos" (1977, Macondo Ediciones)
"Parque de Diversiones II" (1979, Macondo Ediciones)
"Robotobor" (1980, Crea)
"Obras Completas" (1980, Ediciones Corregidor)
"Araminta o el Poder" (1982, Crea)
"Paginas de Marco Denevi seleccionadas por el autor" (1983, Editorial Celtia)

"Manuel de Historia" (1985,   )

BIBLIOGRAPHY ABOUT MARCO DENEVI:

Alegria Fernando: "Novelistas Contemporaneos Hispanoamericanos" (1964, Boston, D.C. Heath and Company)

F.L. Cinquemani: "Rosaura a las Diez" (1964, Dec, 15 "Library Journal")

Coleman Alex: "Rosaura a las Diez" (1964, Oct. 25 "New York Times")

Concha Edmundo: "La novela Latinoamericana de Hoy" (1973, Edicion del Autor, Santiago de Chile)

Gonzalez Eduardo: "Rosaura a las Diez" (1956, No 242 Sur")

House Laraine R.: "Myth in the work of Marco Denevi" (1977, Maryland University, United States)

Leward H.E.: "Ceremonia Secreta" (1965, "Hispania" Dec. No 959)

Llopis Rogelio: "Rosaura a las Diez" (1964, "Cuadernos Hispanoamericanos" No 27, Madrid, Spain)

Mudrick M.: "Rosuara a las Diez" (1965, "Hudson Review" No 110, New York, United States)

Revel Grove, Ivonne: "La realidad calidoscopica en la obra de Marco Denevi" (1974, Mexico, D,F. B. Costa-Amic)

Yates Donald: "Marco Denevi: an Argentine Anomaly" (1962, "University of Kentucky Foreign Language Quaterly" No 3. United States)

Yates Donald: "Introduction" to "Rosaura a las Diez" (1964, Scribner's 1964, pp XIII-XV, New York, United States)

"Tamburlaine The Great of Persia" (Translated by Alberto Manguel, a short story by Marco Denevi, 1985, "Descant 50" Volume 16, No 3, Toronto, Canada)

Piña Cristina: "Marco Denevi; la soledad y sus disfraces" (1983, Essay, Buenos Aires, Argentina)

DOLORES ETCHECOPAR

S he was born in 1956 in Buenos Aires. The daughter of Josefina Castro and Maximo Etchecopar, a Lawyer, Historian, and former Argentinian Ambassador to the Vatican and Consul in Egypt and England.

From the age of 5 she travelled extensively with her family due to her father's diplomatic career. The family went first to Sweden, and this was followed by 2 year stays in Peru, Mexico, Colombia and Switzerland.

Back in Buenos Aires Dolores finished her secondary school and begun her studies of literature at the University of Philosophy & Literature in Buenos Aires. This was interrupted at the age of 18 when she travelled to Switzerland. There she stayed and entered the University of Philosophy & Literature in Geneva. After studying for 4 years she left and went back to Argentina. Her return coincided with the publishing of her first book of poetry "Su Voz en la Mia". Shortly afterwards she went back to Switzerland and stayed in Zurich. There she married Raul Vielma, a Chilean nuclear scientist and remained for 2 years more.

In 1983 Marco, her son was born. In 1984 she returned to Buenos Aires for good. In 1985 her second book appeared "La Tañedora" and in 1986 she published "El Atavio".

Her poems have regularly appeared in many of Argentina's main newspapers: La Nacion, La Prensa, La Gaceta de Tucuman, among others.

Her work have been critically praised and published in many literary magazines: Ultimo Reino, Editorial, Empresa Poetica, Hora de Poesia (Spain). Some of her poems have appeared in Italian magazines; and "La Tañedora" will soon be published in Germany.

Dolores now lives with her son in Buenos Aires. She is preparing a new book of poems. She paints intensively and does cover illustrations for poetry books.

Her poetry shows a distinctive and unusual vein that is close to surrealistic expression. She manages to be highly personal and handles the world around her with a much forgotten lucid finesse. She remains one of the best examples of the new generation of poets in Argentina.

DOLORES ETCHECOPAR
Buenos Aires, 1985.

Soon after I arrived in Buenos Aires, Silvia and Chacho Llanes, some friends of mine, gave me a book to read. The title was "La tañedora" ("She who tolls the bell") a volume of poems by Dolores Etchecopar. The recommendation: to read it carefully. As Chacho and Silvia are the owners of one of the better book stores in Buenos Aires, and in the past we exchanged books frequently, I took them up on their advice. What was strange or rather revealing, was Dolores Etchecopar's book.

That same night I couldn't close my eyes until I had finished it. Next morning I re-read some of the poems and was startled. A new and fresh voice talked with exquisite sensibility about themes that, thanks to the language, revealed a strange familiar territory.

With self containment and some modesty, Dolores' poems opened up a light zone of open spaces and an interior dialogue with the surrounding world ("with emotion", as Borges wished). A poetic world shaped to bring in the smell of the land. Something geographically near to us all, yet so foreign to urban dwellers, not only of Argentina.

But these are not literal depictions of the country and even less of so called "poesic gauchesic" (gaucho poetry). Nothing could be further away from Dolores" poetry. Nevertheless in her work, the presence of nature, the land, water, horses, wheat fields "transfixed to the poetic world" – as she says – are precisely the elements she most frequently names. But perhaps quite uniquely, these elements acquire a dramatic and fantastic presence that is absolutely new in Argentinian poetry. Dolores Etchecopar has published until now three books of poetry: "Su voz en la mia" ("His voice in mine"), "La tañedora" ("She who tolls the bell") and "El atavio" ("The dress/attire").

With these three volumes she has ceased to be "promising" and has become one of the best exponents of the new generation of Hispanoamerican poets.

In her apartment on Ayacucho street – in one of those fine old buildings with slow, wood-panelled elevators – we walk through the living room and the library (books and more books, floor to ceiling) and her paintings (subtle watercolours of dreamlike images and femenine figures dancing).

She has lived and travelled through numerous countries. One of the most recent was Switzerland. Her return to Buenos Aires "for good" makes me ponder on the common experiences of living abroad, and how it affects one.

Dolores has a joyful and somewhat melancholic presence, with delicate features, long blond hair and deep blue eyes. A certain absent-mindedness mixed with a good sense of humour. It is contagious and makes me smile every time I recall our conversations in Buenos Aires.

The Argentine critics have been eloquent in their praise of her poetry. And now she embarks on the fearful stage of being translated into other languages. Something that will happen soon in English.

"In poetry, language is what is said. There is no way of separating language from content" says Dolores. These lines from a short poem of her's are a good example of this:

> "entonces un niño
> tumbo con las manos dormidas de los arboles
> una tierra de oro
> para bajarla al corazon de los muertos".

> "so a child
> with the trees' sleeping hands felled
> a land of gold
> and bore it down to the heart of the dead".

* * * * *

Galvez: Dolores, where were you born and why do you write poetry?

Etchecopar: I was born in Buenos Aires, but can't say why I write poetry, it seems to be unanswerable. I don't know why. It always seemed inevitable. Like the only space offered to confront the human condition, which is incomprehensible. One confronts it with death, time, childhood and love. But why that bond through words?..

Galvez: In our previous conversations, you always mentioned death. Why?

Etchecopar: It's one of my re-current themes. Maybe it's not so tangible in my first books. But yes, death is the originator that propels me to write. It is in the confrontation with death, where any other form of language fails. Most of all, the discursive language articulated by the world, fails. Confronted with that failure there is only poetic language left. And it is anti-language in a way, because it starts where the others leave off.

Galvez: Are the other sorts of language explanatory tools?

Etchecopar: Discursive language is essentially that. It is ruled by logic and an explanatory intention; it leads to objects or to a decipherable message.
In poetry however, "the medium is the message". There is no way to separate language and content.

Galvez: It is then *what* you say, even when it's inexplicable?

Etchecopar: Yes, because something explicable is something that can be said in different words. Poetry has to deal with the inexplicable. It can only do so, through it's own language.

Galvez: Do you write poetry because you need to explain?

Etchecopar: No. I think I've given up trying to explain anything...

Galvez: (laughs) It's a necessity...

Etchecopar: The necessity of creating a new order. A poetic order. An order that can uncover a world of myths and private sensations. Perhaps one born in remote times; and sometimes poetry can restitute that life. But there are never explanations...they are more like a presence in themselves.

Galvez: I know there's nothing worse than asking a poet what she means.

Etchecopar: (laughs) Oh, yes. It is destined to fail or it's a parallel path that hasn't to do with poetic writing.

Galvez: How long have you been writing poetry?

Etchecopar: Publishable, not so long. But I've been writing poetry for ever; since I began writing I always imagined myself writing poetry. Not prose or novels or anything else. But publishable poetry, since I was nineteen.

Galvez: Why do you say... publishable?

Etchecopar: Well, I mean with a certain value, objectively speaking if I can. I think all the other were more personal alchemies, with no value beyond themselves.

Galvez: But now you have brought out this book entitled "Su voz en la mia" ("His voice in mine"). Is it the first one?

Etchecopar: Yes it is.

Galvez: And the second one following it is "La Tañedora". They are both exceptional, especially the second one. It means that you have burst out with two "publishable" books, that are quite out of the ordinary.

Etchecopar: Thank you, but I don't know... I can't say that. I know they are publishable, but have my doubts.

Galvez: You've been writing poetry for a long time and were born in Buenos Aires in the year...

Etchecopar: Fifty six...

Galvez: ... and studied here in Buenos Aires. Then you went through Liberal Arts but were ticked off with the Catholic University...

Etchecopar: Very much so, yes. (laughs)

Galvez: ... and you have the intention – we hope – of writing poetry and what other projects?

Etchecopar: Well, for the time being, I have another book of poems to be published. (the book has already appeared and it's entitled "El atavio" (The attire/The Dress).
But I don't know until when I'll be able to write poetry. It's something that you can't control with the will alone...

Galvez: Those two books: "La tañedora" and "Su voz en la mia" are partially self-financed, as has been the case for dozens of Argentinian writers with their first books, from way back.

Etchecopar: Yes. Sometimes not only the first ones. Unfortunately that's the way it is. And who knows for how long it will remain like that. Because as long as the Argentinian economy remains like this, I don't see how that disgraceful situation for writers can be modified.

Galvez: Yes, we don't know. Even when the economic situation in Argentina was more brilliant, some writers had to finance their books. Take the case of Borges and others.

Etchecopar: Yes, they did. So it is not new here... (laughs).

Galvez: It is interesting to notice that in Argentina there have always been excellent writers. Women writers and even more so, women poets...

Etchecopar: That's true, Alejandra Pizarnik for example, lately.

Galvez: Like Alejandra Pizarnik... and they are practically unknown.

Etchecopar: Yes. It is really terrible it's like that. Especially in the case of Alejandra Pizarnik, who is a great poet. She is better known in France, though, because I've been in touch with French writers and they know of her. The general public doesn't know her, the poets do. In Spain it's the same, I believe. I don't know about other Argentinian writers.

Galvez: Unfortunately very little is known. At least in Canada. They're not known, except in the academic circuits by people who specifically study Latinamerican literature. The result I guess, of what was called the Latinamerican boom. That's fine, but sometimes its detrimental because Argentinian writers have a very specific view point, and it's a pity that it gets lost somehow... Borges is perhaps the only one who is well-known.

Etchecopar: Yes, it is a pity... and Cortazar?

Galvez: Cortazar perhaps, a bit. But poets...

Etchecopar: There should be a way of improving that.

Galvez: Translating them. Publishing in bi-lingual editions perhaps. Promoting them. That would be a good way.

Etchecopar: Yes, that would be ideal of course.

Galvez: What non-Argentinian poets and writers do you like?

Etchecopar: In general? I have liked various poets along the way, according to the needs of that moment. There have been poets who have responded to those needs better than others. So I am an unfaithful reader. But in this moment, I am reading a Catalan poet very fondly whose name is Salvador Espriu. I didn't know him and he is a great poet.

Galvez: Did you discover him here?

Etchecopar: No. In Switzerland, by chance, at a bookstore where they have Spanish books.
He is contemporary. He died, but he is from this century. He is a very secretive poet. I suppose he doesn't have good distribution, but he is a classic. A great poet. The panorama is so big and I've liked so many...

Galvez: But is there someone with whom you feel a special affinity?

Etchecopar: Yes, many. At a certain period I very much liked Saint John Perse. Later, when I started writing, I fell in love with Garcia Lorca of course, and lately I've been re-reading a lot of Paul Celanne...

Galvez: Garcia Lorca, yes. I had a curious experience trying to spontaneously translate Garcia Lorca poems to a Canadian friend. She wasn't exactly a reader... and she thought it was very funny. Hilarious actually... (laughs).

Etchecopar: She didn't like it at all?

Galvez: I believe she couldn't grasp the images. She thought they were absurd...

Etchecopar: But why?

Galvez: I don't know, perhaps the translation, the mental composition...

Etchecopar: Well, there is a difficulty in the poem's translation, but that is very curious. Because I would say he is a poet who is very close to us; who shines very easily. Not like others who require a sort of initiation into poetry plus the habit of reading...

Galvez: Do you like any particular movement...surrealism for example?

Etchecopar: Yes. I believe surrealism is one of the greatest movements of this century.

Galvez: Why surrealism and not any other?

Etchecopar: Because I think surealism is one of the open answers to contemporary man's situation. A man who has lost every orderly horizon...

Galvez: And a sense of the transcendental?

Etchecopar: I don't know if he has lost it, but in any case, that horizon doesn't appear anymore in dailylife.
There is a separation from the intimate world of dreams and prayers; creation and the surrounding world. There is an insurmountable separation which makes the language the world transmits inadequate for the inner life. Surrealism found a way of inventing another language that breaks all the springs of logical discourse, to give place to that interior world.

Galvez: Yes. It relates to the oniric as well...

Etchecopar: That's why, yes. With the subconscious. Con-fronted with the loss of that mundane horizon, man has recourse to an interior landscape which is his subconscious. That is one of the sources of poetic writing.

Galvez: Is it a source of inspiration or something on which you draw freely for your poetry?

Etchecopar: I use it a lot. I try to let it flow so that I can interfere afterwards...

Galvez: I don't remember who said: "Write subconsciously and edit consciously." Is that how it is?

Etchecopar: Yes, the intervention is very important. There is rigour and objective validity that a poem has to have. That's as important as the subconscious source. But obviously the subcon-scious flow has to be there. It has to have a place. Afterwards you can do whatever you want with it; but you can't start with the conscious level alone...

Galvez: You have to leave the door open...

Etchecopar: Of course.

Galvez: You talked about rigour. Are you disciplined in your work?

Etchecopar: Unfortunately I don't have all the time I would like. I have a child and have to care for him. But I try to write frequently even when I don't write anything particular. I try to write a couple of hours a day, sometimes at night. Lately I prefer the mornings. They are more serene. The daytime hours give you the proper distance in what you write. Night time is more intoxicating but also more deceptive. You believe you've written a great thing, until you look at it in the clear light of day. (laughs)

Galvez: Do you throw away a lot?

Etchecopar: Yes. A lot. Many times I suppress an entire poem and only one line survives. Sometimes it re-appears later on another poem. I modify things a lot.
If I didn't publish I would probably correct endlessly. Publishing stops me from correcting on and on...

Galvez: Do you think there's a difference between male and female poets?

Etchecopar: That's long subject, isn't it? But yes, I believe you can see some specific male and female types in writing. But when the artist writes, I believe he is androgynous. In that sense, the artist achieves a wider universality in what he says. If not, it would be writing for women or for men.

Galvez: But there is a stamp...a trade mark...

Etchecopar: Yes, nevertheless there is a stamp. In any case, one of the two characteristics, stands out. Which is the femenine one? It could be a different sense of the poem's body. An immediate connection between the tragic substance of human destiny and the body. It's as if both things weren't whole. In many cases, masculine writing is more conceptual and has a tendency to establish different categories between the bodily and the spiritual. In women, perhaps you get more of a unity between both.

Galvez: Women unifies both worlds more?

Etchecopar: Unifies both worlds more, probably in the best examples.

Galvez: Due to her female condition perhaps?

Etchecopar: Yes. I believe in women, the love theme and eroticism, desire, are more central and impregnate her more than man. That sometimes appears in writing too.

Galvez: Because she can carry another person on her womb?

Etchecopar: I don't know if it's only that. Maybe, as that is a part of the biological fatality. But I'm not sure that is the most intimate part of women. In fact I rather suspect it is the nuptial theme. Perhaps, the union with the other. That "other" could signify the universe, nature or world itself.

Galvez: If I asked you if poetry were necessary...

Etchecopar: Necessary for whom?

Galvez: For everyone. For artists and others. For someone in Buenos Aires, Toronto, the slums in Rio...

Etchecopar: Oh yes. Not only do I believe poetry is necessary but also, art in general. Painting; any activity that is poetic at its centre. The world needs an opening that helps to repair man's desintegration, which is produced by all the potential destruction surrounding us. It needs to repair, as you mentioned before, that sense of the transcendental. That loss can prove deadly to man. After all poetry, as with art in general, is a religious activity...

Galvez: Do you think we live in a secular world?

Etchecopar: Yes, I think the world has become quite secular, and there is a great suffering brought about by that secularization. But suffering brings on important modifications. The artist can create moods in his works where that loss, can be repaired in some way.

Galvez: That's true. Murena (Argentine writer) said that the artist played as the mediator. He talked about nostalgia for other worlds...

Etchecopar: The mediator, yes. I believe that's the way it is.

Galvez: On the other hand, certain poetry or certain poets have become almost unintelligible.

Etchecopar: Yes, I believe that. There's a kind of poetry that seems to be only for poets...

Galvez: Elitist?

Etchecopar: I think so.

Galvez: But it often happens. There's a little group of people that discovers the waltz. After that discovery it expands to wider circles until it becomes popular...

Etchecopar: It should be like that too. It shouldn't remain in a small circle. It would be impossible for poetry to reach everybody from that starting point. Poetry today, has a long history that renders inaccesible at first sight. That doesn't mean it's deliber-ately hermetic. I think good poetry does not have that same tendency. But it might be hermetic in spite of itself.

Galvez: Yes, in some poets it becomes too cerebral and loses it's freshness...

Etchecopar: Yes. Good poetry shouldn't loose its freshness. It is a mutilation when it becomes too cerebral. It's simply bad poetry. Freshness is one of the essential elements of poetry. It's one of the things that differenciates it from other liguistic forms, that have an explanatory intention. Poetry blooms anywhere and without justification. Which gives it freshness and innocence, if we can talk about innocence...

Galvez: We were talking earlier, about your father Maximo Etchecopar (Argentinian Historian-Essayist-writer) and the way he influenced your world. Was your father a diplomat?

Etchecopar: A very special diplomat, because before everything else he is an intellectual. He has been always most at home in a library, with his books, and he was the window towards the unsheltered world, for me. He was the person who showed me how to love literature, ideas, books... without trying to, because he is not a "didactic" person or someone who will impose anything on you. Those things came quite naturally to him and he couldn't breath in other circles.

Galvez: So it's contagious.

Etchecopar: Yes, a healthy contagion. (laughs)

Galvez: And your mother?

Etchecopar: My mother meant a lot in my early childhood. She is an artist. An artist in the raw sense, because she is instinctive and spontaneous. She always painted, very shyly, because she didn't dare propel herself nor vaunt herself as a painter or anything like that. But she always wrote children stories, made drawings, worked her tapestry for hours, and had a strong sense of visual beauty.

Galvez: Aesthetics...

Etchecopar: Very much so. But she is not connected to the world of culture in the broader sense.

Galvez: It seems frequent among certain Argentinians. My mother was somewhat similar. Perhaps for that generation, being a professional artist was simply unthinkable.
Etchecopar: Of course. It was disgraceful, something that was looked down upon. Which implied an immense ignorance. I think the middle class in other countries, for example, were quite

opposite. They knew what art was all about... Here, there was a kind of superstition against intellectuals and artists, as if they were...

Galvez: A plague.

Etchecopar: A plague to be avoided.

Galvez: Yes. And your father opened the windows...

Etchecopar: Yes, wide open. (laughs) And I'm really grateful for that. Because if not, perhaps destiny would have taken away the freedom. Because unltimately that is freedom, not to be attached to a little world with it's own claustrophobic rules, but to have that window open to the outside world.

Galvez: Is that why you write essays? Because that's another world again.

Etchecopar: Yes, in prose, that is probably what I would like to do. I have written very brief things and I'm very interested in that field.

Galvez: It's always interesting to find a poet who writes essays...

Etchecopar: It is very frequent, isn't it? But sometimes different fields have common affinities. As it is frequent the bond between poetry and painting, perhaps even more than between poetry and novel.

Galvez: As part of a new generation of Argentinian poets, what do you think about Borges?

Etchecopar: Well, he is so well known that it's almost impossible to talk about him...

Galvez: Perhaps too well known... for example in Canada, but I mean in the sense that other Argentinian writers are not known...

Etchecopar: One is never "too well known" (laughs). But yes, perhaps it is a bit disproportionate. To me it is a bit inexplicable the huge distribution that Borges has. There are so many writers who could have been similarly recognized and they don't... It seems to me inexplicable also, because in my case, he hasn't been a strong presence in my readings or the authors that have fed me.

Galvez: Perhaps it seems to me Borges is not very representative of the Argentinian psyche.

Etchecopar: I don't know if I agree with you. I think he is, even to the extent of saying he is a product of the Rio de la Plata region.

Galvez: A product of Buenos Aires, yes. But I sometimes wonder if someone from another province, for example Corrientes or the Southern Santa Cruz, would recognized himself in his work or would be interested in Borges. I have the impression he is rather a sort of abstraction of Buenos Aires...

Etchecopar: Well, Buenos Aires is itself a great abstraction. To that extent he is representative of Buenos Aires but not – as you said – of Argentina as a Country. Nor Latinamerica...

Galvez: What happens is that really, Buenos Aires is a very special city and a very strange one in the Latinamerican context.

Etchecopar: Yes, it is an island.

Galvez: That traps you...

Etchecopar: That traps you and has the power of islands. Something very unreal also, as if it is frozen in time... it has a certain charm...

Galvez: A great charm and curiously it is full of characters and little myths...

Etchecopar: Yes... it is as if each one is inaugurating his own universe. It's a world that allows for other worlds, isn'it?

Galvez: And in your poetry, what role does Buenos Aires play?

Etchecopar: I don't know up to what point, it directly interferes with my writing. But it probably does. Over all as a feeling of permanent unreality. Perplexity towards the world that Buenos Aires favours due to what we were talking about. Then, the flat landscape and the countryside adds strength to my poetry.

Galvez: Why?

Etchecopar: Because my childhood happened partly in Balcarce, in the province of Buenos Aires.

Galvez: How many hours is that away from the capital?

Etchecopar: Five hours by car.

Galvez: And what is the landscape like?

Etchecopar: It is a landscape that is not typically of the Pampas, but it has some of its characteristics: the vastness, the distant horizon. But it is less flat. My contact with nature comes from then and there. With the water, the wheat, sky, horses, that so often appear in my poems. All that, nevertheless of course, doesn't have a descriptive sense in my poetry, but it is transposed to a poetic world.

Galvez: Did you just spend summers in Balcarce?

Etchecopar: Mostly summers. The ones that are so important in childhood, because they are the times for vacations and the adventures you live through.

Galvez: Did that continue throughout your life?

Etchecopar: No, it was interrupted around the age of twelve, when I made the first trip to Colombia. I had been in Mexico and other places before and also other factors entered my bond with nature...

Galvez: Were you in the countryside in Colombia?

Etchecopar: No, in the city. But Colombia is a landscape that emerges with a very real force, even in the cities. The presence of rains, of a certain cosmic monotony, that gave me the feeling of what Latinamerica is in general...

Galvez: Latinamerica, generally speaking, is something that Northamericans have confusions with. And perhaps that's the way Latinamerica is: a mixture of tropics, jungle, rain, with the artic in the south. They don't imagine for example, the tip of Argentina at the opposite pole to the Canadian. Sometimes they think it is all a big jungle. Or that Latinamerica is a big country. In Toronto for instance, there are people from Colombia, Ecuador, Chile, Peru, etc. and one has to explain sometimes, that these people are from different countries. They don't come from the same place. They share the same language but not the same geography...

Etchecopar: Nor culture...

Galvez: With some similarities of course, but...

Etchecopar: Of course, yes. But as with every error, the image they have, has its own truth. Because one can't say that Latinamerica has the same diversity of cultures as there is in Europe or other continent. There is a unique historical presence that pervades each country; while Mexico, Peru or Argentina, with all their distinctive nature have different roots.

Galvez: Except for Brazil, we inherited religion and language from Spain after all.

Etchecopar: And we are young.

Galvez: But despite being young, despite Europeans who come to Buenos Aires saying that everything is still to be done here, there is a certain atmosphere – perhaps typical of Buenos Aires – of age and antiques... a certain air of decadence if you like.

Etchecopar: Absolutely. It is like a big abandoned stage set. And that is what gives it a certain magic. All that youth inside a scenario that doesn't exactly fit that youth... there is a sort of dis-encounter.

Galvez: Yes. Plus the fact that half the Country's population lives in Buenos Aires and its suburbs. It's another of the Argentine contradictions. How do you see what's happening now in this country, with the new democracy coming after the military?

Etchecopar: I have to make great efforts to see it. I see it with great pain. Because what Argentina went through under the last military government is something so horrible, so lacking in any kind of human dignity, that it seems to me something that society could not absorb. Therefore, that weight is still there, floating like a nightmare; and I don't know how Argentinian society can integrate that episode and keep going forward. On the other hand, I see the terrible economic crisis. It is hard to imagine how that can be solved.
Now, along with this sombre panorama, I'm very happy we now live in a democracy. I believe it's the only alternative we have and there is no other option. And in that sense, I'm optimistic.

WORKS BY DOLORES ETCHECOPAR:

"Su Voz En La Mia" (1982, Ediciones Corregidor, Buenos Aires)
"La Tañedora" (1984, Editorial El Imaginero, Buenos Aires)
"El Atavio" (1985, Editorial El Imaginero, Buenos Aires)

SILVINA OCAMPO

S ilvina Ocampo was born in Buenos Aires in 1906, the youngest of six sisters. From childhood she draws and paints. Later, she studies painting in Paris, with Giorgio de Chirico and Fernard Leger, following her mother's ambitions for her. Disillusioned, due to frequent misunderstandings with her teachers, she stops painting for a while, and starts writing in secret. It takes some time before she does it openly.

In 1931, her sister Victoria publishes the first issue of SUR, and Silvina's first poems and stories are published there. In 1934 she meets Adolfo Bioy Casares and the next year she illustrates his first novel. They are married in Las Flores, province of Buenos Aires, in 1940, and soon after they decide to take off and discover the "real" Argentina. Together, they buy a trailer and take Ajax, their favoury Great Dane along. Her first book "Viaje olvidado" appears and later she prepares "Antologia de la literatura Fantastica" with Jorge Luis Borges and Bioy Casares.

In 1941, again with Borges and Bioy Casares, she selects the "Antologia de la Poesia Argentina". In 1942 she publishes the poems "Enumeracion de la Patria". That same year Ajax dies. She depicted the dog in "Los dias de la noche", where she wrote a moving portrait of him.

In 1945 she wins the Municipal Prize of Poetry for her book "Espacios Metricos". The next year "Los sonetos del jardin" appear.

In 1946, she publishes the thriller "Los que aman, odian" in collaboration with Bioy Casares and in 1948 "Autobiografia de

Irene" a collection of short stories. The following year they take
a long trip together. In New York they meet up with her sister
Victoria and travel to Europe, principally through France, England, Switzerland and Italy. That same year "Poemas de amor
deseperados" is published.

In 1953 she receives the Second National Poetry Prize for
her book "Los Nombres" and the following year her daughter
Marta is born. In 1956 she decides to write for the theatre and
does so in collaboration with Juan Rodolfo Wilcock. Together
they bring out "Los Traidores". In 1958 she writes a children's
play that opens in the Liceo Theatre under the title "No solo el
perro es magico". The following year "La Furia", a collection of
short stories, is published. In 1961 she writes another short story
anthology "Las invitadas" and the following year she wins the
First National Prize of Poetry for her work "Lo amargo por dulce".

In 1966 she publishes the anthology "El pecado Mortal" and
in 1970 the book of short stories "Los dias de la noche". The same
year her anthology "Informe del cielo y del infierno" appears in
Venezuela, and following that, her book of poetry "Amarillo
Celeste".

In 1974 she publishes a children's story "El cofre volante",
and appears an anthology of her short stories in France, with an
introduction by Italo Calvino and the preface by Borges.

In 1976 the children's story "El caballo alado" appears, and
the next year the book "La naranja maravillosa". In 1979, the
poetry books "Canto Escolar" and "Arboles de Buenos Aires"
appear. That same year her sister Victoria dies in Buenos Aires,
leaving behind the SUR collection legacy, her houses – now public
museums – and a life devoted to Argentinian culture.

From then on, several of her stories are adapted for television and cinema. ("El Enigma", "La casa de azucar", etc.). In
1984, "Paginas de Silvina Ocampo seleccionadas por la autora"
appears. In 1985, her translations of more than 500 Emily Dickinson poems, are published in Spain. In 1987, Tusquets publishes
her short story collection "Y asi sucesivamente", also in Spain. In
1988, Penguin Books Canada publishes "Leopoldina's Dream", a
collection of previously published stories now translated into
English by Daniel Balderston.

Silvina Ocampo writes every day, and lives with her
husband Bioy Casares in Buenos Aires, Argentina.

SILVINA OCAMPO
BUENOS AIRES, 1987

The interview with Silvina Ocampo, started through Bioy Casares' gentle help. "Silvina is difficult" he said "but I'll do my best to make it happen". From then on several things occurred to me. Silvina not only dislikes interviews, but she also doesn't like to talk, and even less with a tape recorder present. What she likes best is playing. And we certainly did play. I was only able to put the material together alfter those games were through. It was a fun period of several weeks, with several intermissions, that took us through the Buenos Aires winter.

There were many telephone conversations, visits to her house and talks we didn't record, and some directly into English "because it's such a beautiful language" that resulted in a couple of hours of tape.

Some nights, as thunder and lightening stormed outside, we sat comfortably in the living room, joined by Adolfito, her nick-name for husband Bioy Casares. Some others were spent by candle light because of power cuts. This gave a particular tone to her smiling complaints of "I find the written dialogues increasingly difficult". But of course, this was not taken very seriously, and she was the first one to laugh.

Other nights, at dinner time, a woman would come to ask her advice about the correct temperature for the chicken in the oven. "Who cares about the chicken" she would say. Then complicitly, she would whisper "I'm sick and tired, you know, of being watched and told what to do...". She was referring to a couple of women who take her health much more seriously than she does herself.

During one of the breaks when we didn't talk, Silvina had a terrible fall and had to be put under intensive care. Nobody knew what would happen despite Bioy Casares comment "the doctors are astonished by her lucidity". A few weeks later Silvina was up as if nothing had happened. She was then, even more gently watched and would even more rigorously dismissed the care. "It was a silly fall" she later said laughing, and continued with her every day life.

Sometimes at sunset, her favourite time for get togethers, she discussed the speed of the american cinema, dismissed Buenos Aires' street life as incomprehensible, praised the wonders of the most simple flowers and plants – including the mysterious ombu – and casually talked about her gift of clairvoyance.

The big apartment on Posadas street doesn't have any heating problems. But for a good number of Buenos Aires residents, the lack of gas during the winter, makes the heating, a chronic problem. Pondering the old recourse to fire places, she would say "Yes, that would be fantastic. But of course you can't get wood easily in Buenos aires. And when somebody finally gets it, there's a strike of course, of I don't know what union, and you can't get matches...". she would laugh and while Adolfito talked, she would silently draw pencil sketches on her lap. She would be annoyed at certain of his smiling remarks, and finally gave me two pencil portraits of myself. "You have a cheeky face" she would say smiling "with something of a taxi driver and perhaps a bit of a Cheff". The portraits, with another one she gave me "the angel of good luck", I have now framed as they are much more than a precious memory.

Silvina draws today, with the same passion of her childhood. "Each time I pick up a pencil my heart beats differently" she said. Oil paintings sparced through the apartment, of Adolfito, children, flowers and dozens of her drawings, confirm this.

In her large and light study overlooking the Mitre park, Silvina comes and goes searching for papers and manuscripts. In the middle of the bohemian order, there are piles of books, unfinished sketches, paintings and an upright piano. We sit on a small sofa overlooking it all. Today she is over eighty. When she takes off her dark glasses, one sees her penetrating and big clear

eyes. The somewhat absent impression she gives, can instantly
reverse to warmth with innocent overtones. Her paintings and
drawings reveal refined simplicity. Her poetry and prose shows:
the musical precision of a writer that, perhaps like anyone elso,
has reconciled the invisible and ambiguous threads that flow
through her characters and the world. She has written incessantly since the publishing of her first book "Viaje Olvidado" in
1937, to the present. Twice awarded the Argentine National
Literature Prize, innumerable other prizes have rewarded her
works. The circumstances and feelings of her characters, bereft
of false sentimentality, are exposed and brought to life through
her sensitivity. These characters, we should add, are unmis-
takebly Argentinian. People who bridge the line between the
prosaic and opaque. In the hands of a less gifted writer, such
characters would fall into simple vulgarity. Not with Silvina
Ocampo. For her, vulgarity, the common place, tackiness, and the
apparently trivial, are occasions to reveal the fantastic.

Her humour, that is innocent sometimes, while corro-
sive at others, is linked to a chaste view found in all her
fiction. A chastened view that is not falsely modest but refined. And that "suggests" the unspeakable, with much more
force than today's abused explicitness.

Her love for French and English, simultaneously learned
with Spanish, propelled her first to fervent reading and later
to translation. Among many others, she has translated Emily
Dickinson, Baudelaire, Verlaine, Alexander Pope and De Pierre
de Ronsard into Spanish.

With Borges and Bioy Casares she compiled "Antologia
de la Literatura Fantastica" and "Antologia de la Poesia Argentina". To Bioy Casares she has been married since 1940.
To Borges she was a long life friend.

Today, Silvina keeps writing as she says "on any piece
of paper I find; in the most uncomfortable positions, over my
knees..." with a similar intensity. She still lives – despite her
love for Rome – with her husband in the Posadas apartment
in Buenos Aires. Ajax and Diana, their favourity dogs are long
gone, but there are others. All the flowers, plants and wonderful trees of Buenos Aires belong to her.

"Y asi sucesivamente" (And so on) is a good example of
her strength, spirit and way of looking at the future. It is the
most recent of a series of books to be published by Tusquets
Editores is Spain.

* * * * *

Galvez: Silvina, what was your childhood like?

Ocampo: Oh, terrible, terrible. I was very sensitive. Horribly sensitive, and noone realized it...

Galvez: Noone?

Ocampo: No. Probably because I was very quiet.

Galvez: And that's a sympton in itself...

Ocampo: Yes, but they never thought of interpreting things like that. Maybe one starts to lose intelligence, don't you think?

Galvez: I don't know if you can lose it...perhaps one loses sensitivity.

Ocampo: That for sure. One becomes perturbed by other things. Because you don't handle sensitivity as you do in childhood. There are people who believe a child doesn't feel anything. That he is like anyone else...

Galvez: Or that children are not aware...

Ocampo: It's because they haven't been children. Or perhaps they were, but they don't remember. Or they forget how they were. They are 20 or 30 and don't remember their childhood at all...

Galvez: You had five more sisters, and probably most of them were extremely sensitive...How come your parents didn't notice?

Ocampo: No.   I believe they didn't.   I got the worse deal...(laughs)

Galvez: Why?

Ocampo: Because it's horrible to be very sensitive. It's fine to write, create, paint or make music, but not for living. Life unfolds in a more and more vulgar, rude way. As they discover things like this... (she points at the tape recorder) to replace people. People will talk with these instruments...(laughs)

Galvez: Some people think that in this era of computers and visuals, books are destined to disappear. Do you believe it?

Ocampo: But one never knows what can happen. Something magical may occur. The book could suddenly appear and start following you...(laughs) It could have an incredible power of attraction and start following you. I hate papers yet I'm surrounded by them. I could destroy them all. And suddenly, of course, I would be left with nothing of what I've written. How aweful..! (laughs)

Galvez: Maybe you should use a computer...(laughs)

Ocampo: Oh...one could have a computer inside oneself. Do you have one inside? (laughs)

Galvez: Well, finally, the brain is a computer...

Ocampo: Of course, yes. Nothing is unique. They invented the computer because of the brain, if not they couldn't have invented it.

Galvez: A few years ago, I was watching a documentary about William Penfield, a famous Canadian neuro-surgeon. They were showing, in open surgery, how a patient's brain was stimulated by electrodes. When they touched specific zones, the person responded to music. She would remember a forgotten melody from childhood. She was of course under local anesthesia. They would then stimulate another part of the brain and the lyrics came back...

Ocampo:: The lyrics and not the music...That is precious!

Galvez: The documentary ended saying that nowhere in the brain could they detect a zone that gave a hint of the soul...(laughs)

Ocampo: (laughs)...it's true.

Galvez: You said that you suffered much in your childhood, how did you manage with your sister and friends?

Ocampo: I wasn't sociable. I've never been sociable. I didn't need to be with people. I didn't like parties. They would iron my plaits. I let them do it and my hair looked so nice, everybody said: "what a lovely hair this girl has!.." (laughs) Did you like parties?

Galvez: I guess I was a total contradiction. Because really what I would have liked was to be invisible. That's what I've would have liked...

Ocampo: Oh yes! Me too! What a marvel to be invisible! It was the most wonderful thing, wasn't it? But one never could, and when you had to be there, you worried. But to be invisible, my God!

Galvez: I've read somewhere that you said you were not sociable but intimate. I believe that happens to many sensitive people. You can't have a conversation with more than one person...

Ocampo: It is difficult. It requires a lot of practice, But how could one do it: You could never be yourself in front of 20 people. In the first place, the voices are bothersome, because all of them are quite different. Some on top of the others, some silent. You don't have any quiet peace to hear them. So you don't hear them anymore. One hears the sound they produce, but not what they're saying.

Galvez: When we were children, we used to hear a lot of songs in English. I heard the lyrics but never paid attention to the meaning. It was a matter of how they sounded with the music...

Ocampo: Yes, because that is the main attraction. The sound, the voice saying something. But also, the expression one gives to words and phrases is very important. That's why people reading poems, read them so badly. It seems they are not saying what it is written anymore.

Galvez: Silvina, why do you write?

Ocampo: I write so I do not have to talk. That's the truth. I don't like to talk, but I like to write. I have something written

about that I can give you, if you like. It's from a french magazine.
(What follows is Silvina's written answer to the magazine) "I
write so that others love what they should love, which is sometimes what I love too. I write so I don't forget friendship and love,
wisdom and art – the most important things in the world. A way
of living without dying, a way of dying without dying. Something
from ourselves and our souls remains on paper. It's something
that escapes life and which is more important than the voice that
is modified by health, luck, rhumatism, deafness and finally by
age. So what's left of the world? Sentences instead of voices,
sentences instead of photos. I write to forget my scorn. I write
so I do not forget, out of hatred, anger, love, regret; so I never die.
I write on my knees, on my arm, on paper, on a magnolia, on a
pane in my window, on the background of the house where noone
comes, on the rump of the marble horse that carries me into the
clouds of the sky. I write to change destiny, so that life takes over.
Above all I write so I don't have to speak. There are monkeys
and dolphins that speak. Instead of praising them we crucify
them. I write so that the memory, that sooner or later we lose,
becomes the main objective in life. I write so that when one
speaks of the rose, it lasts for all ones life on pink or green paper.
I write the name of my dog so that he doesn't die as he died so
sadly. Writing is a luxury. I therefore write to be happy, since
I am unhappy without real reasons. To express myself, to rejoice,
to lose myself, to find myself in my complicated pain or my
rainbow joy. Palinure (pilot of the Aeneid) exists and writes. He
sleeps on my heart as on the blue of the sea. Andersen's mermaid
has a wonderfully written voice. The guardian angel in my
lauguage is more beautiful than in life. Listen to him when I call
him through my writing and not in my horrible spoken voice. I
write so that I am loved, so that noone says that I lie; for it is only
in writing that one says what one thinks and not when speaking
of what doesn't interest us. Let's rejoice that we can write
throughout our lives rather than always having to speak of things
we do not know. Like the bird that repeats the same phrase a
thousand times just to be applauded. Writing is the thing I most
love in life; then, like an overly sweet dessert that I don't really
want, I draw the glowing wonders of earth with the same pen.
Writing saves me from everything, it's my lifebelt when sea and
river waters are about to drown me. Each time one wants to die,
one loves oneself. One seeks a touching way of saving oneself,
so one writes a prayer to God on the sand or on a stone. Then
one feels one is not lying even though one seems to lie along with
Palinure, the mermaid and the guardian angel. One always
posesses truth when Joan of Arc is being burned. Joan of Arc
heard voices. What did they say? We shall never know. But we

never forget them. So I have lied. Please forgive me those who have read me through the mystery of voices, in the fire perhaps, or in the most celestial light of struggle." So that's why I write. To be loved. Because I think I can't be loved. If I write I know that what I'm writing will get to the soul of someone. I don't mind who it is...

Galvez: Is it not important to you to see faces or to hear responses?

Ocampo: After a while, yes, I can see them. But while I write I'm not thinking of...or perhaps I will think of a friend of mine, yes. "I'm going to write this because he will laugh or he will love it, or he'll think it's really clever of me." But not always. There is always a person who is unknown, but one can imagine him as if you knew who he was.

Galvez: You mention that you like to write anywhere...on your knees...

Ocampo: Yes, yes, always! And the more uncomfortable the better...

Galvez: So, do you search for uncomfortable places to write?

Ocampo: No. They appear suddenly. It could be a piece of paper that's not very white or clean. I start to draw on that. And I could do my best things on it. If I have some beautiful paper and I see I could do something on it...well, it's a pity because after that, the paper is no good anymore. It's horrible! I have drawn horrible things because I've tried for very nice things. I've been too careful.

Galvez: Was it always like that?

Ocampo: Yes...it's very mysterious. When I go to sleep, my husband says: "Why do you curl your legs up?". Well, perhaps I was very happy like that. It reminds me of those people who ask for money in the streets...

Galvez: Beggars?

Ocampo: Yes. Perhaps I am a sort of a beggar... (laughs). I once wrote a poem on beggars. When I was a child in San Isidro, many beggars would come to the house. Now you have beggars in Buenos Aires. But at that time, all the beggars at a certain day of the week would come to the garden. And I thought they were beautiful. They had long, very red hair. Their faces were brown and they didn't walk like ordinary people. They had broken legs, black eyes. Everything was broken down, but I thought they were wonderful. And so I used to talk with them. But when they caught me, I was told it was wrong to do those things. Because... why did I like to talk with beggars?

Galvez: Well, you have a wonderful long poem call "Michele", inside a book about San Isidro written by your sister Victoria...

Ocampo: You know, I can't remember that one...you've got the book?

Galvez: I saw it in a Library. It is called "San Isidro" by Victoria Ocampo. It has a collection of photographs by Gustav Thorlichen and a long poem called "Michele" who is a beggar. There's a picture of him on the railtracks, near the river...

Ocampo: Well, you must show me that book, please...

Galvez: I will, of course. Silvina, a couple of days ago we were talking about your love of painting and music. Those were strong forces inside you. When did you switch to writing?

Ocampo: I wrote a lot as a child, but only the teacher saw what I wrote. And she didn't think I wrote well. She thought I used too much paper to do it on. I used to scribble the most incredible things. Letters, words that you couldn't pronounce, it was terrible...(laughs) I thought that it was very difficult to write correctly, and so I tried words. The most incredible and awkward words. And so the reader had to look for a language that was quite odd; Russian or something. Not English or Spanish.

Galvez: And probably not even French. You started writing in French or was it English?

Ocampo: Both at the same time...

Galvez: And Spanish as well?

Ocampo: Yes. But I didn't like Spanish. I hated Spanish at a certain time. English seemed like something magical...it was beautiful the English lauguage...

Galvez: Yes, it still is...

Ocampo: It still is, but I have lost it. I don't practise as I
used to. Now, I can't pronounce the words well, they don't come
easily...

Galvez: Perhaps it's only lack of practice, and like drawing,
you will come back to it quickly...

Ocampo: Yes. And I used to love drawing. Since I was a
child, it was very special for me. I drew all the time. Even when
my mother didn't want me to have the lights on in my bedroom,
I drew with no lights and with my eyes closed. I have done many
drawings like that. I will look for them to show you...

Galvez: Was this long ago?

Ocampo: Not so long ago. I once thought "how awful to lose
ones sight" and I started drawing with no lights on. And I could.
Noone knew that those drawings were done that way.

Galvez: And did you always draw things from imagination?

Ocampo: No. When I was 7 years old, I had a teacher. My
mother wanted me to be a great painter. She always thought that.
And I used to draw the faces that I saw. I did portraits. I would
tell the person "I'm going to do a portrait of you'...and the person
would laugh...

Galvez: You promised me one...

Ocampo: Yes...but you are not laughing...(laughs)

Galvez: All right...(laughs)

Ocampo: I used to play in a park where some Japanese
people came. They were little children. And a Japanese man took
them to play there. I started to draw them. And so the man came
to me one day and asked "what are you drawing?" "I'm just
drawing" I told him. "No, but what is it that you are drawing?" he
said. "Well" I told him "I was just drawing everything I see. That's
what I've been told to do and that's what I'm doing". "Give me
that" he said "you can't draw my children". "But why can't I?" I
replied. He didn't answer because he didn't know Spanish well
enough. He went away with my papers and I saw him tearing
them apart. He was furious...(laughs) He thought I have done

something terrible, drawing his children. And the children were very beautiful...

Galvez: It's like the stories of the Indians and the photographs...

Ocampo: Yes, exactly...

Galvez: Silvina, earlier we were talking about angels...and you have a book "Santoral" that relates to that...

Ocampo: Oh yes, the angels. They taught me to love the angels very much. This was very important for me. Some of the angels were very pretty. The ones I saw in churches were much nicer than the one's you see now. I don't know what happened to angels. They are not as pretty as they used to be when I was a child...(laughs) I used to give them my soul when I went to bed at night. And I told them "I give you my soul, would you please give me something better?" I believe they were very good to me, sometimes. But sometimes, I forgot them. And I thought that I would never be happy. Yes, that's what I thought.

Galvez: But why did you think that?

Ocampo: Because I started to tell lies to the angels...

Galvez: (laughs) Why?

Ocampo: I lied to them really. Because there were things that I had to tell them. And as I didn't think I lived very well, I told lies. I thought I wasn't a child like the rest. I used to tell them things and they didn't understand...

Galvez: The other children, you mean?

Ocampo: Yes. And I would say "but why don't you understand what I'm telling you?" and the answer would be "because I don't understand". Well, I was telling them things that were very inconvenient for a child.

Galvez: You learned that afterwards...

Ocampo: Yes. I knew everythings I had to know before I was six. I knew a lot of things. How did I know them? I was very curious, and as I was very silent, noone knew that I was looking at everything...

Galvez: What a combination, silence and curiosity...perhaps frightening.

Ocampo: Rather frightening. I thought so much. I was always thinking. I always thought of God. I was always thinking about God. I even doubted if He lived or not. If He existed or not. Because I wondered "why is everyone lying to me? I know there is chocolate there and they are hiding it. Then they told me God lives. He can't live. He can't exist..." That's what I thought when I was a child. And then I wanted to kill myself because of all those thoughts. It was horrible. It seemed terrible to doubt.

Galvez: No wonder you couldn't exchange notes with other children... did you get along with adults?

Ocampo: No. I had nothing to do with them. They were much older, and this was at a time when women were supposed to look like ladies. They never looked much at me. So when I was growing up, I thought that I would look like an old person too. I didn't want to grow up, but I was much older than the other children...

Galvez: You didn't go to school...you had a teacher...

Ocampo: No, I didn't go to school...

Galvez: So your teacher, must have been wonderful...

Ocampo: No. None of my teachers were wonderful. I had one that was very nice, an English woman who came to live in the house. We were in San Isidro. She came from England and she didn't know a word of Spanish...

Galvez: So nothing but English all the time...

Ocampo: All the time English. She wasn't much of a teacher, but I liked her in a way. I liked her and hated her too...

Galvez: Were you an easy child?

Ocampo: I think I was pretty good...I was spoiled I suppose. But I use to punish myself...

Galvez: Silvina, what about the translations you've done?

Ocampo: Yes, I have enjoyed them a lot. Overall because

translating means to lift something away from you. It is giving yourself to a text that is not yours, but that you make your own. That's how I have translated. Everything that I have translated, I've done it as if it was my own. So I thought that what I was doing would be useful.

Galvez: You translated Emily Dickinson...did you choose by affinities?

Ocampo: Well, when I first read Emily Dickinson, I like her very much. So I began to translate her. I liked her, but then I realized that perhaps she didn't deserve such adoration. Suddenly she would have a poem that moved me very much. I translated them with all my soul. But little by little, once they were done, I began to feel cold about her. I started to feel that way, because sometimes I founded things from Emily Dickinson among my papers, and I would be angry. Among the things I had written there were her things. And I would say "But it's not possible, I'm not going to write like this! I can't write like this!.." And so in that way I was mistaken. But, one always make mistakes...do you like her?

Galvez: Yes, very much.

Ocampo: She is very good and I like her writing much. But suddenly, it's like going back in time...

Galvez: And ones tastes change...like "the blue period", "the yellow period".. Who else did you like translating?

Ocampo: Well, I liked translating the French poets. I thought they were splendid. I also liked the English. And felt relieved when I found things that I enjoyed and could also translate.

Galvez: You translated Baudelaire...

Ocampo: Yes, I did several things from him. In some of my last books, there are translations of Baudelaire...

Galvez: And Nerval...Did you like him a lot?

Ocampo: I have done some things from Nerval also. Yes, I liked him. Not as much as the others, but nonetheless I liked him...

Galvez: Translating is such a difficult and subtle art...

Ocampo: Yes, but one feels free of so many other things. Our own self, specially. One has such a big responsability in writing. But translating is something that helps a lot. And it helps because it's a fine exercise...

Galvez: Did you like Rimbaud, did you like Verlaine?

Ocampo: Rimbaud, yes a lot. And Verlaine. I translated quite a few things from Verlaine. But I found out that he was almost impossible to translate, because Verlaine seemed written in Spanish. I mean, I saw it almost in Spanish. So some poems I did well. But the other ones, the ones I felt sounded like Spanish, came out naturally. Have you ever tried to translate Verlaine?

Galvez: Not really. I don't know French enough to do that. But I tried translating some poems of a friend into English. From Spanish to English; with a friend of mine whose mother tongue is English. She and I worked separately on the same poem and then chose the best of both. It worked out quite well...

Ocampo: Oh, how good...

Galvez: Yes, in the end I believe it's a labour of love, is it not?

Ocampo: Of love, yes. Of giving oneself. One renounces oneself and translates something, doubting and doubting, but hoping for the best. One is capable of working on a translation for days and days, only for the desire to give oneself to something. And not remaining within oneself.

Galvez: Do you believe Rimbaud was the phenomena people say he was?

Ocampo: I think Rimbaud has very beautiful things. I don't remember any poem by him, do you remember any?

Galvez: The beginning of one: "One day I sat beauty over my knees and found her bitter..." from "A season in hell" (Une saison dans l'enfer)

Ocampo: It's beautiful...

Galvez: I like him very much. The thing is that reading him is sometimes, like reading a storm...(laughs) a marvellous storm...

Ocampo: It's true. Because there is such an accumulation of words and ideas inside Rimbaud's poems, and everything is so beautiful, isn't? But Verlaine is so good. What Verlaine has is such a simplicity in what he has written. In the composition of his poems. A magnificent simplicity. Each time I found Verlaine more perfect.

Galvez: Silvina, could you not write?

Ocampo: No. I couldn't. Sometimes one asks oneself "would I be able not to do this, or not to do that?" I think I wouldn't be able not to write. Because I believe that writing is like the salvation of the soul. I don't want to use that word, soul. It is like a protection that there is inside us, against everything selfish and useless. It is everything that seems to take us a bit nearer to heaven. It is something that can redeem us in a way...

Galvez; And if you didn't write, would you paint or make music?

Ocampo: I would paint, probably. I would paint with great fear. Because all of the arts are muddled up with a series of horrible things that one has to go through...

Galvez: You mean, art got muddled up with horrible things?

Ocampo: Yes.

Galvez: Are you refering to the commercial aspects?

Ocampo: Yes. All that world in which everyone tries to make money...it's horrible. Horrible I think! When I started painting I was about seven years old. I hadn't touched a pen yet. But I swear you, painting was a terrible necessity. It was so much so, that when I started painting my heart would beat in a very special way...I felt I was going to meet my love or something that was very important for me. And today I'm still the same way. I may have lost strength, I can lose new ideas, I can lose myself in that world without balance or equilibrium, but I feel my heart beating differently when I draw, or when I'm going to write something. Or even when I think of an idea. A poor little idea, that perhaps is not so poor. If I write it down, it means it had some worth for me. That's how it is.

Galvez: An intact sensitivity...

Ocampo: Yes, I think that's what I have the most of, sensitivity. It is the only thing that saves me...

Galvez: Sensitivity and intelligence, that's what Adolfito (Bioy Casares) was saying the other day; that sensitivity on it's own, without intelligence, doesn't work. Both things always belong to good poets and writers.

Ocampo: Yes, I believe so. I think they have to be together. But, I don't know what to do...

Galvez: What you're doing Silvina...(laughs)

Ocampo: To die perhaps; for the things that one feels should become reality. I thought many times about death. When I was a child, when I was so tiny and samll, I thought about death. All the time. And in this last book I talk about death. I don't think anyone will like it...

Galvez: The short stories? ("Y asi sucesivamente") But why? It's one of the most important themes of life...

Ocampo: It's important, but it's a theme I don't think people like...

Galvez: It's not commercial.

Ocampo: That's right, it's not commercial. That is the disgrace...

Galvez: But at the same time, today, that's probably a guarantee. If it's not commercial then it must be good...(laughs) If one could exercise any form of art and avoid that parallel world, it would be ideal...

Ocampo: It would be lovely. But what a danger. What a danger to be threatened by those things growing around us. I believe they're suffocating us.

Galvez: They are everywhere, and with particular enthusiasm in cinema, for example...

Ocampo: I am divided between cinema and painting. Cinema attracts me very, very much. I think I could be capable of doing films...But I don't know if I have shown in some way, the capacity to do it...

Galvez: But of course! First, you have the visual aspect; you paint. And for the screenplays, you have your writing. So you have the two basic ingredients. And then, you also have music, which means rhythmm.

Ocampo: Exactly, without rhythmm you can't do anything in cinema... Oh, I would love to do films! Wherever I am waiting for something or someone, I always imagine scenes for films... But there is a backward movement in films. I've seen little of the new cinema apart from American thrillers. I don't like them, but nonetheless, they do them well. They have good timing, among other things...

Galvez: Yes. But you haven't really missed much lately. In the past 10 years there haven't been many excellent films. Although there is a Russian director, Andrey Tarkovsky, who has superb films. Especially one called "Andrei Roublev". The best I've seen in years. The film happens in Moscow -- it's the Tartar invasion in the 1.200 aprox in black and white. It is magnificent. Shot in 70 mm, with an incredible rhythmm and photography...

Ocampo: Tell me, and the timing is good?

Galvez: Very good. It is slow, because the Russians have that timing. Slow in comparison to the American that is very fast. Too fast sometimes. But the slow pace in this film was required by its theme...

Ocampo: Do you think is a mistake, that obsession with speed that the Americans have fallen into?

Galvez: I think is due to the anxiety they have with instant gratification...(laughs) They want everything *now* and *fast*...

Ocampo: Yes, what horror. I remember when I was in the States. I went to eat to one of those drugstores. I sat, very innocently, at the table... and instantly they put a plate and instantly they asked me what I was going to eat. The open menu came immediately, everything, and then immediately I was obliged to eat. They asked "Is this okay or you want something else?" I replied "No, I don't want something else, how could I, if I don't know what this one tastes like?"...(laughs)

Galvez: So he wouldn't serve you?

Ocampo: No. Finally he wouldn't serve me...(laughs) So I started looking for someone else...I went to the States as a visitor, for a month. I was in the middle of New York.

Galvez: Did you like New York?

Ocampo: No. Not immediately. But I know that I'm slow to get a liking for a city. And furthermore, everything was such in a hurry...with the food...(laughs) So don't think that I liked it very much. I thought that if I stayed and lived there, then I was going to like it. I like things when I stay long enough. But when I first arrive to a place, I don't like it...

Galvez: You need time. But you liked Rome...

Ocampo: I liked Rome very much, yes. I loved it because I like the time there. It is a time that flows. That flows naturally. You can feel it inside you, and that is similar to where you have lived. There is no change. You fall into a lovely country, with lovely things, and so you don't feel homesick, although it's a bit difficult...

Galvez: Yes, I'm going to Rome, for the first time, next year. For a short period...

Ocampo: It's very nice to go like that, passing by. Because in that way you are not going to have that feeling of arriving in a city, and missing everything. No, no, you're not going to miss anything. Everything will feel familiar to you. Rome is so beautiful...

Galvez: And not like the monstrous size of Buenos Aires. I suppose it's intimate...

Ocampo: An intimate city. Intimate and it doesn't make you waste time. You can't get lost there. You arrive anywhere easily. Its such an exquisite city. I assure you there's nothing I like more than Rome. I would also very much like you to go to Florence. Florence is a divine, divine place...

Galvez: Silvina, what about influences, which writers or artists have influenced you, if any?

Ocampo: (laughs)...I don't know what to tell you...well, I think Kafka had an influence on me...

Galvez: Did you admire him much?

Ocampo: Very much...and you?

Galvez: I did. But he had something I didn't like much. That implacable logic that anguished me and at the same time his lucidity...

Ocampo: Did he anguished you much?

Galvez: That nightmarish feeling was a bit heavy on me, yes...

Ocampo: Oh really?

Galvez: Yes. But I did like him.

Ocampo: I liked Kafka because he always surprised me. All the time he was surprising me. And that continuous surprise left me in awe...

Galvez: I enjoyed very much his book "Letters to my father", that you've probably read. It was marvellous.

Ocampo: Those letters yes, wonderful. I liked the book a lot. But I felt that Kafka's capacity to surprise people was natural in him. It wasn't a pose. He never seemed to be re-working anything, never. I liked that. It seduced me. And I have the impression that things ocurred to him immediately. He would start writing and already he was saying astonishing things. Amazing things that were really very simple. He would bring out amazing things from a piano, a chair, anything he touched...

Galvez: Who else did you like?

Ocampo: For me, besides Kafka...its difficult. Because for me, he was a prodigy. Of course, there are others. Sometimes when I read now, I discover things that I enjoy a lot in other writers. And I think how wrong not to have read them before. But then, one doesn't have the time to read so many things...

Galvez: And what Argentinian writers?

Ocampo: Well, I liked Borges very much. I really liked him. But Borges sometimes repeated himself, overall in the last years. I liked him a lot, nevertheless. I liked his prose more than the poetry. I don't know, reading his poetry I felt he was retaining himself. I didn't feel he had freedom. It didn't seem he was writing with freedom and that bothered me a bit. But I understand this was a mistake of mine, to notice that that way of writing didn't correspond to the fear he had...

Galvez: But what you're saying is true. Perhaps it was the risks of a writer in his desire for precision. And this could result in a certain coldness...

Ocampo: Yes, yes. And too dry suddenly. A dryness that shouldn't remain in the text. I think this dryness shouldn't be in Borges' writings. Because Borges wrote very beautiful things. And he felt very beautiful things. But suddenly, there was something that made him withdraw. Wasn't it the fear of ridicule?

Galvez: Perhaps it was. Certainly he was a man of an enormous contained emotion. And sensitivity.

Ocampo: Oh yes, I believe so. And one can never rid oneself of that contained emotion. Never.

Galvez: Is writing fantastic stories, in the sense of "fantastic literature" unavoidable for you?

Ocampo: I think it is unavoidable...for now. But I hope some day it won't be so. Because I would like to free myself from that...

Galvez: It sounds as if you're trapped...(laughs) in any case, if you are, it's seems a very interesting prison...

Ocampo: Well, that consoles me. I like it. It gives me a bit more tranquility and peace of mind. If not, I feel that what I write goes too far into the fantastic...

Galvez: It does. Sometimes it goes too far away, but that's fantastic – in both senses –. And that's one of their attractions. Because if not we could end up with the so called "realism"...(laughs)

Ocampo: (laughs)...yes, what a horror..."realism"...(laughs)

Galvez: Because so called "reality" cannot be documented truthfully in any case. Not even with a photograph. What projects are you involved now?

Ocampo: There is a project for a film, directed by Christensen, based on a story inside a story I wrote, called "The house
of sugar" (La casa de azucar). It will be a sort of co-production
with Brazil, because Christensen lives there. But the arrange-
ments had been going on now for a long time, and I don't know
when they are going to start filming.

Galvez: Did he write the screenplay?

Ocampo: Yes. Before that, he did a film here that was a
scandal. I can't remember the title now. It was based on a short
story by Borges, and it's about two brothers who fall in love with
the same woman. That is Borges' story. And Christensen has
put them both in bed making love...the two of them...

Galvez: The two brothers? So that was his invention...

Ocampo: It seems it is in the short story. I think it's a bit
strange, but I don't know, I'll have to read the story again. So this
was a very difficult situation, and Borges and Christensen had a
fight. Borges said he had never written that...So with all these
things, the screenplay has been postponed many times. Christensen told me he worked very hard on it. In any case, why would
I like to know when it is going to be made really?

Galvez: What is the story of the "House of sugar"?

Ocampo: It's the story of a couple who are very much in
love and they want to get married. She insists on searching for
a house in which noone has lived. She doesn't want to get married
before they find it, because she hates the idea of living in a house
where other people have lived. They search everywhere, until
they find a nice white house, in which it seems nobody has ever
lived before. At least, that's what the future husband tells her. It's
a pretty house. So they decide to buy it. And the film starts when
all the wedding guests go to the house to congratulate the couple.
Many things happen of course. Someone starts phoning, insisting
on speaking to the woman who used to live in the house. They
tell him it must be the wrong number. Nobody by that name lives
there or has ever lived there. And so the story unfolds. The film
was done here and it opened in Buenos Aires last year. I think
it was well done. So what they want to do now is another film
that takes part of that story.

Galvez: So you liked the film version...

Ocampo: I saw it on a video cassette. And it wasn't bad at all. The main character was well portrayed. I can't remember the actress's name, but she was good, I liked her. She didn't overact.

Galvez: What about the screenplay "The impostor" that you wrote?

Ocampo: "The impostor", yes. I have it somewhere. I really like that one.

Galvez: When did you write it?

Ocampo: A long time ago. It's about a young man who goes to an abandoned estancia (Argentinian ranch) to study. He is tired of people and wants to live alone for a while. The only people there are a house keeper and the husband helping her. So he lives there for some time. But one day another young man appears and starts talking to him. And here the mystery begins. The new arrived listens and discusses all his problems with him. While there, the young man studies constantly. He reads Greek literature and all sorts of beaufiful things...

Galvez: So, the other young man who talks to him, is half spirit, half real?

Ocampo: Yes, he's a sort of an angel. But one day his arrival is announced...

Galvez: You mean the same fellow who was talking to him?

Ocampo: Yes. A bit strange isn't it..? (laughs) Yes, but I'm not telling the rest. It's a pity I can't find it now so I can read some parts to you. I think you would like it. But I don't trust my memory. It has plenty of dialogue and plenty of silence. There is also a girl he had fallen in love with, and she lives in a small village near the estancia. But she falls for the other young man as well, and finally she goes to the estancia...

Galvez: I like the idea and I guess the estancia has to be really something...

Ocampo: Oh, I can't tell you what a wonderful place it is! It is called the swan lake, because there is a lake near the house, where there used to be swans. There is a terrible but beautiful scene in which he decides to kill the swans, because he believes they're bad luck. And so he does. But you'll read it when I find the screenplay...

Galvez: Silvina, the titles of your books are very interesting...

Ocampo: You think so?

Galvez: Yes...

Ocampo: Why?

Galvez: Well look..."Almost the reflection of the other one" (Casi el reflejo de la otra), "Earth sheets" (Sabanas de tierra), "The fury" (La furia) they catch ones attention...

Ocampo: Well...(laughs) at least they do that...(laughs)

Galvez: Yes...(laughs) speaking about "The fury", was that book dedicated to Octavio Paz?

Ocampo: Yes, I dedicated a poem to Octavio Paz because he dedicated one to me. It is called "Mirando el Sena" (Looking at the Seine) which is inside the book...

Galvez: Did you see him when he was in Buenos Aires last year?

Ocampo: Yes, I did. He is a very good essayist and I like what he does very much. Not so much his poetry, but I like him.

Galvez: Silvina, how do you see the future?

Ocampo: Which one?

Galvez: (laughs)...Yours and everyone else's.

Ocampo: (laughs)...Well...aside from death I don't know what it could be... I see it being so confused. It seems to me like those big pots someone is stirring with wooden spoons... I see everything stirred up, and you?

Galvez: Me too. But with little light appearing at the bottom...

Ocampo: Really? Oh how lucky...that you can see that little light. I can't see it. But I can tell you that I am praying all the time.

Yes, I swear to you I'm praying. Because it seems that everything is fading away from me. That everything is disappearing. That the world is turning dark. Dark as if the lights have been turned off...I hope what I'm telling you is not true...(laughs)

    Galvez: Me too...(laughs)

PRINCIPAL WORKS BY SILVINA OCAMPO:

(Original title, year of first edition and publishing house. Unless otherwise noted, all originated in Buenos Aires, Argentina).

"Viaje Olvidado" (1937, Sur)
"Antologia de la literatura fantastica" (1940, Sudamericana) (Collaboration
    with Borges and Bioy Casares)
"Enumeracion de la patria" (1942, Sur)
"Espacios metricos" (1945, Sur)
"Los sonetos del jardin" (1946, Sur)
"Los que aman, odian" (1946, Emece) (Collaboration with Bioy Casares)
"Autobiografia de Irene" (1948, Sur)
"Antologia de la poesia argentina" (1948, Sudamericana) (Collaboration with
    Borges and Bioy Casares)
"Poemas de amor desesperado" (1949, Sudamericana)
"Los nombres" (1953, Emece)
"Pequena Antologia" (1954, Ene)
"Los traidores" (1956, Losange) (Theatre. Collaboration with J.R. Wilcock)
"La furia" (1959, Sur)
"Las invitadas" (1961, Losada)
"Lo amargo por dulce" (1962, Emece)
"El pecado mortal" (1966, Eudeba)
"Los dias de la noche" (1970, Sudamericana)
"Informe del cielo y del infierno" (1970, Monte Avila, Caracas, Venezuela)
"Amarillo celeste" (1972, Losada)
"El cofre volante" (1974, Estrada)
"El tobogan" (1975, Estrada)
"La naranja maravillosa" (1977, Sudamericana)
"Canto escolar" (1979, Fraterna)
"Arboles de Buenos Aires" (1979, Crea)
"Paginas de Silvina Ocampo seleccionadas por la autora" (1984, Celtia)
"Y asi sucesivamente" (1987, Tusquets, Barcelona, Spain)
"Leopoldina's Dream" (1988, Penguin Books Canada) (Translation into English
    of previously published stories)

BIBLIOGRAPHY ABOUT SILVINA OCAMPO:

Andersen Imbert, Enrique: "Teoria y tecnica del cuento", Buenos Aires, Marymar, 1979.

Bengoa, Daniel: "Del juego de la conversacion" La Nacion, 24 Oct. 1982, Buenos Aires.

Bianco, Jose: "Viaje olvidado". El Hogar, 24 Sept. 1937, Buenos Aires.

Borges, Jorge Luis: "Enumeracion de la patria". Sur. No 101, Feb. 1943, Buenos Aires.
    Preface "Noticias de la tierra y el cielo". Paris. Callimard, 1974.

Calvino, Italo: Introduction "Noticias de la tierra y el cielo". Paris, Gallimard, 1974.

Cozarinsky, Edgardo: Introduction "Informe del cielo y del infierno". Caracas, Monte Avila, 1970.

Chacel, Rosa: "Los que aman, odian". Sur. No 143, Sept. 1946, Buenos Aires.

D'Elia, Miguel Alfredo: "Darse en autenticidad". La Prensa, 12 Nov. 1972, Buenos Aires.

Ghiano, Juan Carlos: "Silvina Ocampo y su realidad". Ficcion, No.22, Nov-Dec 1959, Buenos Aires. "La esencia del cuento". La Prensa, 27 May 1962. Buenos Aires.

Gonzalez Lanuza, Eduardo: "Autobiografia de Irene". Sur No 175, May 1949, Buenos Aires. "Eficacia magica". La Nacion. 22 Oct. 1972, Buenos Aires.

Guasta, Eugenio: "La furia". Sur. No 264, May 1960. Buenos Aires.

Grondona, Adela: "Porque escribimos?" Emece, 1969, Buenos Aires.

Hernandez, Juan Jose: "Los nuevos poemas de Silvina Ocampo". La Nacion, 28 April 1963.

Lagunas, Alberto: "Silvina Ocampo y sus aportes al genero cuento". La Nacion, 19 Sept. 1982, Buenos Aires.

Lancelotti, Mario A.: "La furia". Sur, No 264, May 1960. Buenos Aires. "Las invitadas". Sur, No 278, Sept. 1962. Buenos Aires.

Martinez Estrada Eloy: "Silvina Ocampo: la crueldad, la pasion". La Nacion, 10 Jan. 1960. Buenos Aires.

Martinez Estrada, Ezequiel: "Espacios metricos". Sur, No 137, 1946, Buenos Aires.

Mazzei, Angel: "El temblor de lo inadvertido". La Nacion, 27 Jan. 1980. Buenos Aires.

Molloy, Silvia: "Silvina Ocampo: la exageracion como lenguaje". Sur, No 320, Sept. 1969, Buenos Aires.

Noel, Martin Alberto: "Persistente fantasia". La Nacion, 16 May 1982, Buenos Aires.

Paz Leston, Eduardo: "Una antologia de Silvina Ocampo". La Nacion, 22 Jan. 1967. Buenos Aires.

Percas, Helena: "La original expresion poetica de Silvina Ocampo". Revista Iberoamericana, No 38, Sept. 1954. "La poesia femenina argentina" (1810-1850). Madrid, Ed. Cultura Hispanica, 1958.

Pezzoni, Enrique: "Enciclopedia de la literatura argentina". Sudamericana, 1970, Buenos Aires. "La nostalgia del orden". La Nacion, 21 Aug. 1977, Buenos Aires.

Pizarnik, Alejandra: "Dominios ilicitos". Sur, No 311, May 1968, Buenos Aires.

Revol, E. L.: "Silvina Ocampo, narradora magica". La Gaceta de Tucuman, 18 Nov. 1976.

Roggiano, Alfredo Angel: "Diccionario de la literatura latinoamericana". Washington, Union Panamericana, 1958.

Schoo, Ernesto: "Los traidores". Sur, No 243, Nov. 1956, Buenos Aires.

Sola, Graciela: "Silvina Ocampo, la furia y otros cuentos". Revista de Literaturas Modernas". Mendoza, No 2. May 1960.

Trevia Paz, Susana N.: "Contribucion a la bibliografia del cuento fantastico en el siglo XX. Bibliografia Argentina de artes y letras, Fondo Nacional de las Artes, No 29-30, 1966, Buenos Aires.

Ulla, Noemi: "Silvina Ocampo". Centro Editor de America Latina. 1981, Bs. As. "Encuentros con Silvina Ocampo". Universidad de Belgrano, 1982, Buenos Aires.

Villordo, Oscar Hermes: "Donde se encuentra el paraiso". La Nacion, 25 Sept. 1977, Buenos Aires. "Canto escolar". La Nacion, 4 Nov. 1979, Buenos Aires.

OLGA OROZCO

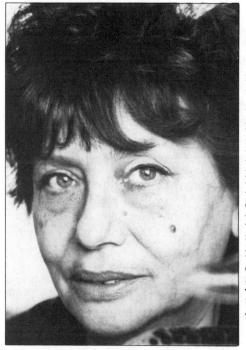

She was born on 17 March 1920 in Toay, a small town in the Province of La Pampa, Argentina, where her father operated a lumber business. Her childhood was spent between there and Buenos Aires. In 1929 her family moved to Bahia Blanca, on the Atlantic coast. There she got to know the sea and the landscape, finished her primary school and started college. During those years she took up violin but said she was a "frustrated violinist".

In 1936 she moved with her family to Buenos Aires and in 1937 she became a teacher, but never practised the profession.

In 1938 she started her Literary studies at the Faculty of Philosophy & Literature. There befriended several talented poets and writers. Among them: Alberto Girri, Daniel Devoto and Eduardo J. Bosco. She published her first poem in the student magazine"Penola".

In 1939 she met Norah Lange and Oliverio Girondo, two of the most talented Argentinian poets and a lifelong friendship began.

In 1940 she joined the group that contributed to the Literary magazine "Canto". With other collaborators, they became known as the "Generation of the 40's".

In 1946 she published her first book of poems "Desde Lejos" and the next year she travelled to Bolivia and Chile.

In 1951 her second book of poetry "Las Muertes" appeared and in the following years she travelled extensively through Brazil, Peru, Ecuador and Chile.

In 1961 she won a grant from the Foundation for the Arts to study the Occult and the Sacred in Modern Literature. For 9 months she travelled through Spain, Italy, France and Switzerland.

Her third book of poetry "Los Juegos Peligrosos" was published in 1962 and in 1964 she won the First Municipal Prize of Poetry in Buenos Aires.

In 1965 she begun contributing to several magazines and newspapers under various pseudonyms: Valentine Charpentier, Carlota Ezcurra, Richard Reiner, Jorge Videla, Elena Prado, Martin Yañez, etc. That same year she was selected to represent Argentina in Paris, under a UNESCO Grant given to Spanish-speaking writers.

In 1967 she published "La Obscuridad Es Otro Sol" a book of tales, and won the Second Municipal Prize for Prose. In 1969 she travelled through Italy, France, Switzerland, Belgium, Holland and England.

In 1971 the Argentinian Poetry Foundation gave her the Grand Honour Prize.

In 1972 she won the Municipal Prize of Theatre with her work "Y el humo de tu incendio esta subiendo", and travelled to Greece and Italy. In 1974 her book of poems "Museo Salvaje" appeared. It won the Second Prize of Regional Poetry. She went through Africa, staying in Liberia, Nigeria, Ghana, Zaire, Angola and also South Africa.

In 1975 her anthology "Veintinueve Poemas" appeared in Caracas. In 1976 she went to Spain and Switzerland and Italy, where the Italian Government gave her a Grant to study the different forms of contemporary Italian poetry.

In 1977 her book of poems "Cantos a Berenice" appeared and in 1979 she published "Mutaciones de la Realidad" (poems) and her "Obra Poetica" (Poetry Works) was released by Editorial Corregidor.

In 1980 she won the Grand Prize of the National Foundation for the Arts, and in 1981 the Esteban Echeverria Prize. She was invited that same year to Mexico by the Inter-American Congress of female writers.

In 1983 she went to Mexico and Peru and in 1984 her book of poems "La Noche a la Deriva" appeared in Mexico. That same year she travelled through Spain, France and Italy, and "Paginas de Olga Orozco seleccionadas por la autora", a selection of her own best writing appeared.

In 1985 "Antologia Poetica" was published in Madrid by the Instituto de Cooperacion Iberoamericana.

Among the many newspapers and literary magazines she has written for are: (Argentina) La Nacion, Clarin, La Opinion, La Gaceta, Sun, Anales de Buenos Aires, Espiga, Davar, Testigo, Oeste, El Litoral, Ficcion, Poesia-Poesia, Nosferatu, Macedonio, A Partir De Cero, Xul, Letras De Buenos Aires, Vigencia, America en Letras, Ultimo Reino, Pliego de Poesia. (Bolivia) La Razon. (Brazil) O Globo, Jornal da Bahia. (Colombia) Eco, Gaceta, Revista de la Universidad. (Spain) Hojas de Poesia, Equivalencias, Cuadernos Hispanoamericanos. (France) Les Lettres Nouvelles, Cuadernos, Liberation. (Mexico) Cuadernos Americanos, Revista de la Universidad de Mexico, Vuelta, La Gaceta, Los Universitarios. (Peru) Las Moradas, Cuadernos Trimestrales de Poesia. (Sweden) Dunganon. (Switzerland) Ecriture. (Venezuela) El Nacional, Revista de la Universidad, Zona Franca. (Uruguay) El Dia. (United States) Via, Alaluz, Escandalar, Hispamerica.

Olga Orozco, considered today one of the most important poets in the Spanish Language, lives in Buenos Aires. She is preparing two new books: "En el reves del cielo" and "Tambien la luz es un abismo". Her poems have been translated in to French, English, Italian, German, Roumanian, Hindi, Portuguese and Japanese, among others. Her work is studied in several universities in Argentina and the United States and she has lectured extensively in many cultural institutions and Universities in Argentina, Bolivia, Peru, Mexico, United States, Italy and Switzerland.

OLGA OROZCO
BUENOS AIRES, 1985

Olga Orozco has huge blue-green eyes, feline and penetrating. An air of astonishment and wisdom flit through them constantly. While we speak and associate mutual friendships, she
comes and goes from the livingroom to the kitchen. She is making
tea, a ceremony that is still celebrated in Buenos Aires – between
five and six in the afternoon. In Toronto, contrary to what the
English tradition might have us believe, it has disappeared.

The large, quiet living room, is on the seventh floor overlooking Arenales street in the heart of Buenos Aires. A large book
case obscures one of the walls. On top of it are some art objects
and paintings. But few things interrupt the carefully aligned
books. Opposite the balcony that overlooks the street, a small
bridge table and a lamp stand in a corner. We sit there and talk.

Among many things we touch upon her passion for astrology and the fantastic. It is a passion she shared with an aunt of
mine and that brings back many familiar stories.

Olga Orozco's name came to my attention then, long before
her poetry and books. And it was always associated with a world
that brought me mysterious echoes and night shadows. This is
the first time that I see her in person. She looks somehow very
familiar.

"I'm interested in all the poets who walk on the edge of the
abyss" says Olga. All of her poetry is really at the edge of that
abyss. Like a constant search, while not being easy, it is not
neither hermetic or obscure. It has a vigorous balance between
metaphysics and the unknown.

Her work, some of which has already been translated into
English, ranks among the most important in the Spanish language.

Since her first book of poetry "Desde lejos" (1946) ("From afar") to "La noche a la deriva" (1983) ("The night astray") going through the stories of "La obscuridad es otro sol" (1967) ("Darkness is another sun"), a theatrical piece "Y el humo de tu incendio esta subiendo" (1972) ("The smoke of your fire is rising") which won the Buenos Aires Municipal Prize of Theatre, "Las muertes" (1952) ("The deaths") "Los juegos peligrosos" (1962) ("Dangerous games") "Museo salvaje" (1974) ("Wild museum") "Cartas a Berenice" (1977) ("Letters to Berenice"), various anthologies and Prizes – among them, the Great Honour Prize from the National Foundation of the Arts (1980) – Olga Orozco has always followed her own voice.

Associated many times to literary movements, surrealism among them, she has never really belonged to any of them entirely. She is faithful instead to an independence of expression, that forces her – stripped to the quick – to be an explorer of the human condition.

Her search is not a despairing one. Without naming dogmas or particular adherences, her search is essentially religious (re-ligare; to unite). With the presence of death – which she considers an integral part of life and not her opposite – and the hope for another life. The other side of the coin. Her search, expressed with an ease as natural as breathing, through metaphors, dreams, magic and myths makes her work doubly interesting and risky.

Her poetry, as a place and preference "where everything is possible" as she herself said in this interview, is transformed through a subtle command of the language, into a place where "other realities" are revealed.

"I play tricks on time" she says. And if time – that convention that we always measure by exterior realities – is susceptible to alterations through imagination and poetic language, Olga Orozco achieves it in her poetry. An omniscient point of view.

A new one that alternates without stumbling between the elements of nature, the "I" who speaks and the spiritual world that embraces them all.

* * * * *

Galvez: Olga, does the fact that you were born in Toay, in the province of Buenos Aires, influence your poetry?

Orozco: I think it does. I think it has a very special meaning, because I was born in the Pampas. A special place, open and wide, where you get vertigo looking at the horizon.
Looking up, also produces vertigo. So one feels sucked in all directions. I believe it also gives you a very special sense of eternity and continuity. Each small object, any plant, every little stone, takes on a meaningful shape.
As if it were the beginning of something; the initiation of an era, of a phase of history.

Galvez: You were talking earlier about your grandmother, and you said she had a lot to do with your work.

Orozco: My grandmother was an incredible person, a mythical being. She influenced me a lot. I was born in the midst of an amazing fantasy world. Julio Cortazar (the Argentinian writer, recently deceased) says for example, that for him "the fantastic" started through his readings, when he was already an adolescent. For me, "the fantastic" was always mixed in with my own life. I had to discern what wasn't fantasy later on. That's probably what made me choose poetry, because it was a place where everything was possible. That's how it had been up to then, in every place my family lived in.
My grandmother gave much more importance to the extraordinary than to ordinary daily things. Not only more importance but extraordinary things didn't mystify her. She didn't need confirmation.

Galvez: For her, that was reality.

Orozco: That was the obvious reality. That was daily reality. She saw the most unbridled imagination as the anticipation of something that you see at a distance. Instead, anything coherent or rational made her seriously doubt it's consistency and reason for being. She inherited this from her Irish mother, who used to tell her stories when she was a child. She was also quite a character. Even 50 years after her death, she came to visit us at home. Very frequently she would visit my sister and I when we were little girls. After 1 p.m. when the lights were off, she came to our bedroom and rocked to and fro in a Viennese chair. When I described this lady to my mother, she would say: "Naturally my dear, it's my grandmother Florencia. She comes home because she loves us very much". As for my own grandmother... there was no need to comment. A little noise as of wings; a movement in the darkness; a vague whisper and she would say: "Don't be troubled my dear, they are ghosts; nothing else but ghosts".

Galvez: Your grandmother was born in Argentina?

Orozco: My grandmother was born in Argentina yes, in San Luis. In a place call Renca.

Galvez: And your father and mother?

Orozco: My father was born in Italy and mother comes from San Luis.

Galvez: Your first book was "Desde Lejos" (From Afar) in 1946. Did you start writing with that book? How does the story go?

Orozco: No, no, I started writing when I didn't know how to write. I was very shy and at the same time, very curious. I always thought that the answers that adults gave me were unsatisfactory. So therefore, my images started interrogating nature about its mysteries. Well, poetry is always an eternal questioning... That's how I started. My mother took notes of some images I would think up; some metaphors doubtless, and when I was fifteen she gave me all the papers. I made a great fire of them when I reached twenty; not only those images but six or seven books that I finished by that time...

Galvez: Why the great fire, you didn't like them at all?

Orozco: It was a great fire... But no, I didn't like them, and

I'm sorry. Although I don't know. My memory has been kind to me; it has been very indulgent and I don't remember anything of that. Maybe some themes...

Galvez: And what did your mother and grandmother think of all that?

Orozco: They always encouraged me to write. They professed a great love for writing and poetry. For anything that was fantastic, and so my world, that was fantastic also, was very much in harmony with theirs.

Galvez: And after the great fire... Did you have some favourite poets? Had you started to read already?

Orozco: I read always. Since I learned how to read and write. I read every night, even when the lights went off, with a lantern between the sheets. Yes, and when I reached twelve, I had devoured all Dostoyevsky, of course. Yes, I've always been a reader. Naturally, I started with basic readings, but I quickly jumped to other realms. So I would read: Garcilaso, Quevedo, San Juan de la Cruz, I read Santa Teresa while I was studying my language; then of course: Rimbaud, Mallarme, Baudelaire, Nerval, and in English, Blake, among others.

Galvez: And you stayed in Toay. Then you went to Bahia Blanca where you continued your studies...

Orozco: I finished primary school and started the secondary in Bahia Blanca. Then I finished secondary school and university in Buenos Aires.

Galvez: You then went to the Arts Faculty in Buenos Aires.

Orozco: That's right, yes.

Galvez: About "La obscuridad es otro Sol" (Darkness is another sun) you say it's not a novel. It was written in prose and won the 2nd Municipal Prize in Buenos Aires in 1967. If it is not a novel, how would you describe it?

Orozco: They are childhood stories. Earlier, you read me a paragraph saying childhood wasn't finished for me. I play tricks on time. Time is something that I carry deep inside; and people, happenings and landscapes mature at the same rate that I mature. I have had periods of carrying things inside, so that they would follow my own happenings. It is a way of violating time. It is what Zorian says when he catalogues this violence, as one of the great adventures that man can have. I play cards with time; intercalating different periods, altering it's continuity and it seems it is a way then of retracing death, of spelling its alphabets in reverse.

At other times, more than these kind of plays, I played with memory, which is what you saw in "Desde Lejos" and "La obscuridad es otro sol". It means taking the happenings with oneself and submitting them to actuality, to the present. Up to the last consequences...

Galvez: How is it that you attached yourself to surrealism, if indeed you did?

Orozco: Well, I don't know if the surrealists directly influenced me. I think the surrealists' predecessors influenced me from afar. They were considered prestigious to surrealism itself. And after that I was always a good friend of the group the Argentinian surrealists formed here. The ones that started "Letra y Linea" (Letter & Line), afterwards "A partir de Cero" (From Zero) later called: "La Rueda" (The Wheel). I can't say I participated in that movement exactly; only collaborated with some translations. I wasn't in the movement itself and I don't consider myself a surrealist but related to surrealism. I was never orthodox. Among other things, I never suscribed to automatism, although I had a lot of elements in common. The exaltation of love, freedom, poetry. The awareness of the different planes of reality without judging them as an exclusively immediate reality, but as a totality. The infinite pirouettes you perform with the ego, until you arrive to its last abysses and possibilities. The unfoldings or double vision - or whatever you want to call them - that muddled world without recurrence to drugs of course, is something absolutely established in my personality and in my writing.

Galvez: Olga, you have won countless awards in Argentina: the 1st Municipal Prize in 1962 with "Dangerous games". The Argentinian Foundation for Poetry's Grand Honour Prize; 2nd Regional Award of Poetry in 1974; the Award from the National Foundation for the Arts in 1980... what do such awards mean to a poet?

Orozco: Well, it means something that is given out, exclusively as a token. But it doesn't weigh for or against the work. And one views it, with a certain amazement... as if it was simply a coincidence between a series of collective wills and judgments...(laughs).

Galvez: Yes, but I think it influences people who don't know much about poetry or read poetry. It encourages people to read, doesn't it?

Orozco: Yes of course. Now, just because I'm saying this,doesn't mean that I believe an award disqualifies one.

Galvez: What does it mean to be a poet?

Orozco: I like the definition that the North American poet Howard Nemerov gives: "To be a poet is to urge God to speak".

Galvez: And poetry?

Orozco: I think poetry is absolutely indefinable. As an extension it would be the same, to urge God to speak. But, you can't define it. It's like the sphere that Pascal and Jordiano Bruno speak of...

Galvez: So, sometimes God speaks...

Orozco: Yes. It's like that sphere, because the centre is everywhere and the circumference nowhere. To try to define poetry is like attempting to catch a dream... It escapes you, it overflows all possible definition. It's always that, and something more.

Galvez: What Argentine poets and what foreigners do you prefer?

Orozco: Well, the most frequent ones from the Argentines, the ones I re-read, which indicates certain preferences and re-lationships, are: Oliverio Girondo, Ricardo Molinari: all people from another generation...

Galvez: You were, or sometimes are associated with the 40's generation in Argentina. How do you see that?

Orozco: I don't believe it was even a generation. I think it was a group of people who reunited to put together a magazine. It's not that I expect a generation to form a school, but we were all of very different ages and tendencies. If you take a look you'll see classicists, neoromantics, intimists; some surrealism. We had so little in common except for a program of staging in a certain landscape, working towards a common ideological truth. I didn't have any need for that.

And if elements of landscape circulate in my poems, it is something that simply was there because I was there, and for no other reason.

Galvez: The magazine you mentioned happened in Buenos Aires. What about the rest of the country?

Orozco: Well, there were some poets from the provinces, from Entre Rios for example: Alfonso Solis Gonzales and Carlos Alberto Alvarez.

Galvez: What other Argentinian poets do you like?

Orozoco: I mentioned to you, from the past generation. I could name Enrique Molina and Alberto Girr, from the present one, for example.

Galvez: And from among foreigners?

Orozco: I'm interested in all the poets who walk in the edge of the abyss. Michaux always interests me, Nerval. Rimbaud interests me... Baudelaire of course! I mentioned him before...

Galvez: Did you like Verlaine?

Orozco: Not so much. Lautremount interests me. The German romantics.

Galvez: We were talking before about the circle of people who buy poetry.

Orozco: Yes...

Galvez: Do you think it's constant or is it that now there is a new generation of young people who are more interested in po-etry?

Orozco: I believe that the number is more or less always the same. Because the slumps that occur among the older ones are occupied by the new ones who join...(laughs).

Galvez: (laughs) The circle re-generates...

Orozco: Yes. But I believe that there are always very few poetry readers. "Poetry as a local poet says – doesn't sell because it doesn't sell". I think it's a lovely definition.

Galvez: Yes, it is a very difficult area. The promotion and convincing people don't matter... It's as if you can't convince them. It happens or it doesn't.

Orozco: And besides, the fervour for poetry is something absolutely untransferable.

Galvez: Do you see essential differences between poetry and prose? It is curious what Borges says about it. He doesn't see them as two confronting worlds.

Orozco: Prose, by force, follows a more linear trajectory than poetry. It seems to be a more coherent path. The construction of a process that is aimed at a specific end or story. Even if poetry has a solid structure, it is not as obvious as it is in prose. It is therefore quicker for people to grasp prose more easily. Poetry demands a much more intimate participation and a greater tension.

Galvez: You mentioned coherence. Is it important for poetry?

Orozco: It is for me. I construct poems like building a house. I can't let the foundations sink, the columns fall down, or the ants take away pieces of the basement or the roof fall in over my head. I build a poem to inhabit it.
I don't like those hybrids that some bad poets, especially bad surrealist poets make, in which "the elbow cries"...for example, or "the eye brandishes a knife". I don't like taking things out of their functions. If the new role they're going to play is not really harmonious and credible, even in the most extraordinary fantasy.

Galvez: So in a certain way, it's not aestheticism nor is it solely beauty but perhaps truth...?

Orozco: No, I don't ask for truth, I ask for credibility. Meaning, I ask for harmony.

Galvez: Form and content together..?

Orozco: No... neither. (laughs)

Galvez: (laughs) What then?

Orozco: They go together. When the creator is really a creator, each one from the start indicates what the other one should be. They are totally fused together.

Galvez: They are indistinguishible then... in the sense that you can't separate one from the other. Or can you?

Orozco: No, of course. It's like a glass of water. It's the same thing. The glass has water, but the water is not the same substance as the glass nor the same shape.

Galvez: What would you say is your central poetic theme?

Orozco: Well, I think that there is a recurrence of certain themes, like death and time. There is a permanent impulse also, to surpass my limits; to penetrate the impenetrable, to touch the invisible. Lately, something is more naked than before. It is something that has touches on Kafka or is related to Beckett in some way. Although there is a biological scepticism in Beckett, that I don't have. I have a certain kind of faith. Certain feelings that the world doesn't end here, that there is an explanation and life thereafter. Walking along this avenue of life before you get to the end, you find yourself unsheltered. In the middle of contra-dictions, always fighting; with a rope between your toes, or against a wall you can't go through. Or a door that mysteriously won't open.   That permanency of impossibilities frequently appears in my poetry.

Galvez: Do you have a favourite work or period in your work?

Orozco: No...you're always interested in the more recent things. I believe a poet is always throwing the same stone at the same target. The stone falls in different ways, but the centre, I believe remains the same. Logically you think with the last stone you got closer to the centre. But maybe it's a false impression. An outsider might judge it better than oneself.

Galvez: What about male and female poets?

Orozco: I don't see any difference. The creative act doesn't have sex. It is a spiritual adventure shared by men and women. Especially in poetry.

Galvez: You don't believe then in feminism in literature...

Orozco: No, not all all.

Galvez: What a relief...(laughs). Your work has been translated into English...

Orozco: Yes, it is included in many anthologies. Recently
there was a whole book translated, and now they're doing another one.

Galvez: How do you write. Are you disciplined?

Orozco: It depends on the circumstances and on the phase
I'm in. Generally though, I write in the mornings because I am
more lucid. At night things seem more attractive but it is defi-
nitely more illusory. In the mornings, it's more real. But I don't
have any special methods. A poem is not born in the same way
each time. Sometimes it is an idea looking for a dress, a cloak
of words. Other times, it is the word searching for something to
live in. It happens in many different ways. What I always have
is a global sense of the poem. I know how it starts and how it
ends. And approximately the path it's going to stroll along. But
nothing else. I never go from the first to the second line unless
I have firmly decided the first one.

Galvez: And what happens when you re-read that poem, do
you recognize yourself?

Orozco: Later on?

Galvez: Yes.

Orozco: Oh, I don't do that.

Galvez: You don't re-read your poems?

Orozco: Never, never. Not even when I have to choose them
for an anthology. I choose them by chance.

Galvez: Oh really?

Orozco: No, it would be like looking at myself in an old
mirror. No. I even try not to look at my old photographs. And
when someone takes my picture... well, sometimes I'm amazed
because I put on the face of who I was, and out comes the face
of who I am. But I just have to recognize myself, because it is the
one of the moment.

Galvez: You have a book of poems "Cantos a Berenice"
(Songs to Berenice) why don't you tell us who Berenice was?

Orozco: Berenice, for the outside world, must have been a female cat. She was my totem. Another me, in a way. She was jet-black and arrived at my house out of the blue. It was a very happy encounter that happened by chance: the kind that is the most premeditated trick of destiny. She had high psychic powers. I think she dictated the best things I wrote during that period. She lived fifteen and a half years. She had furthermore, absolutely magical healing powers. On her palate she bore the black circle, which is the sign of sacred Egyptian animals. She had very curious gestures too, that come from very old traditions: like walking backwards and turning the plate upside down. A common thing in other times, when apparitions occur.

Galvez: She stayed with you for fifteen and a half years?

Orozco: Yes, and after her death she stayed in the house for about ten or twelve months. She would scratch the tables, she would be scratching from inside the wardrobe, knocking off hangers... then she left for good.

Galvez: Do you have the need to write? Could you stop writing?

Orozco: No, I don't think so. I write because I need to, yes. Now I don't have those crazed desires of arriving home, with a beating heart, feeling that the hounds are biting at my heels.
I have felt that, very few times. Maybe I felt like that with the book about Berenice. It was a book that gushed out. But it isn't strange. I was writing it, unknowingly, during the fifteen and a half years of her life. I had then some urgency to write it down so it would not escape me; so it wouldn't fly away.
Perhaps I should see what it feels like to be stopped from writing. But there's something worse than being stopped, and that would be if someone made me...

Galvez: Of course, if you were made to write probably...

Orozco: I couldn't write a single line.

Galvez: What about journalism? You have been a journalist for several years...

Orozco: Yes, for about fifteen years. It was a lot of fun, but my journalism was a bit like research.

Galvez: In what sense?

Orozco: I was in charge of special articles. Biographical writing. Scientific investigation pieces, articles about occultism. Of course, I filled in many blanks too. Sometimes I would write about the difficulties of being a woman today or the silvery colours in fashion. Any topic I was given. But usually they were the long investigative pieces.

Galvez: You mentioned the supernatural... what role does it play?

Orozco: Well, I have a primitive mentality in the good sense of the word. I believe in what Bruel refers to as "the primitive peoples". I have an animistic mentality. I believe in the life of all things, including objects. Therefore, logically, I'm interested in all the nuances. From Astrology to card readings and all the rest. And I have always been interested in it. Even with the little practical sense that characterizes Pisceans (that's my sign). I've studied Astrology in an orthodox way for many years. And I have practically never read a book about magic, that amazes me or that give me new knowledge. I always had the feeling of a re-reading. I must have had previous lives in which I was a participant of one or two of those activities.

Galvez: And as a poet, what paradises and what infernos?

Orozco: I don't know, do you mean favorite ones?

Galvez: The ones that you decide to travel into. As a poet, when you create, sometimes you make a choice. Often there is a dark mysterious world. Is there a recurrence of that world in counterpoint to a world of light or do the two merge together?

Orozco: I think they are opposites, but I believe also that light is an abyss...(laughs). That's the title of a new book. I believe that "darkness is another sun". No, I think that precisely through the word one is making an analogical conversion of the Universe. Each time going further away from where one is. Each time further away to the heights or down to the depths. And little by little, you even lose the notion of the place and time, at the moment of creation. You remain united to the place and to the moment by an incredible thin thread that is almost imaginary. And then, there is a certain panic of not being able to come back. I don't know where you would end up, but it is something that does not bring you back to this side.

Galvez: It caught my attention, after all these years away from Buenos Aires, that there is corruption in the language... Do you think there is?

Orozco: Yes there is. Furthermore, the slang that is invented, gives the impression that it is even more forced, false and ridiculous. Yes, I feel it constantly.

Galvez: Does bad journalism or the media have to do with it?

Orozco: Yes, they always have. Haven't they? Before it was with those absurds circumlocutions and now through some horrible linguistic defects.

Galvez: Do you think poetry is useful?

Orozco: Well, I've always said that poetry is perverse and unhealthy.

Galvez: (laughs) Why?

Orozco: It is unhealthy because it obliges the writer to extraordinary tensions. Those abysms and the difficulties of getting to a determined surface. Those extreme tests with sensations. All of that is unhealthy and perverse. And it's all to get to a specific end. But I believe it helps others because it keeps them company in their sorrows, worries and amazements when confronting the world.
I think it's useful, for poetry talks to the reader at a very intimate level. It increases his hope. It makes him feel that he's not alone. It obliges him. not to go to sleep from comfort. And it can tell him some very tangible and intangibles truths as well.

Galvez: Sabato said: "You don't write to please but to shake".

Orozco: Of course.

Galvez: Is there an essential difference between Argentinian and other Latinamerican poets?

Orozco: I don't think so. You see, in certain regions there is a great variety of tones, so I could say that in a sense, they are more ascetic. But there is a lot of baroque here, as well. Perhaps there is less influence of stormy elements; of an exuberant landscape and nature, but generally speaking, I don't think there is much difference.

Galvez: You don't think there is such a thing as an essentially German, Cuban or Argentinian poet?

Orozco: Perhaps there are, but I don't believe you can make that distinction in Hispanic America. Except in the case of excessively local poets.
Perhaps the case of poets who make use of specific language and traditions...

Galvez: Epics, perhaps.

Orzco: Yes.

Galvez: Your last book was in 1984. Are you working on a new one?

Orzoco: Yes. One that deals with the situations and contradictions of life. The agression and the feeling of being rejected.
I have a feeling of unity; a very deep unity with humanity and the substances of the world. It's as if we were all made of the same matter.
But, I feel there are two movements within me: one of expansion and the other of re-absorption.
The movemennt of expansion leads me to fuse with the outside. I fuse with that unique substance, beacause I feel I'm nothing more than a dot in a circle, a determination in some form of continuity. But I also feel the rejection in some form of continuity. But I also feel the rejection, because the outside has its limits and I have mine. There is a skin in between, and there is a special configuration that is different. So then, a movement of retraction occurs. In this last book, I'm exploring that movement of rejection. The one that obliges me to this retraction.
The expansive movement was expressed in three or four poems in "Dangerous games". They speak about that last unity. Specially in "Everyone's masked unfolding" and "The fall".
It is a very deep religious feeling in the end. Because I believe God is shared among us, through a luminous and invisible substance that will re-unite with Him, when we have perfected ourselves.

Galvez: What do you think about the conflicts that Canadian artists experience with thier search for identity?

Orzoco: I think it is a problem that resolves by itself. We Argintians do not have a very clear definition of who we are either. We should ask ourselves the same questions. Like Canadians, we don't have a tradition that is absolutely ours that will back us, and that we can hold on to. it is probably the same for the rest of the American countries. But I believe that is not a hindrance. To the contrary, it opens up the Universe for us instead...

Galvez: Is it an advantage perhaps?

Orozco: In a way it is. As long as we do valuable things, we are both the tradition and the future; we have both elements within us.

PRINCIPAL WORKS BY OLGA OROZCO

(Original title, year of first edition and publishing house. Unless otherwise noted, all originated in Buenos Aires, Argentina).

"Desde Lejos" (1946, Losada)
"Las Muertes" (1951, Losada)
"Los Juegos Peligrosos" (1962, Losada)
"La Obscuridad es otro Sol" (1967, Losada)
"Museo Salvaje" (1974, Losada)
"Veintinueve Poemas" (1975, Losada)
"Cantos a Berenice" (1977, Sudamericana)
"Mutaciones de la Realidad" (1979, Sudamericana)
"Obra Poetica" (1979, Corregidor)
"Antologia" (1982, Centro Editor de America Latina)
"La Noche a la Deriva" (1984, Fondo de Cultura Economica, Mexico)
"Paginas de Olga Orozco seleccionadas por la autora" (1984, Editorial Celtia, Coleccion Escritores Argentinos de Hoy)
"Antologia Poetica" (1985, Instituto de Cooperacion Iberoamericano, Madrid, Spain)
"En el Reves del Cielo" (1986, Per Abbat)

PRINCIPAL ANTHOLOGIES IN WHICH SHE APPEARS

"Seis Poetas Argentinos" (1946, Cuadernos Americanos, Mexico)
"Poesia Argentina" (1940–1949) (1949, Coleccion El Ciervo en el Arroyo)
"Poetisas de Espana y de Hispanoamerica" (1952, Cuadernos Americanos, Mexico)
"Antologia de la Poesia Universal" (1953 and 1957, Selection by Miguel Brasco, Editorial Castelvi, Santa Fe)
"Antologia de la Poesia Hispanoamericana" (1958, Selection by Julio Caillet-Bois, Editorial Aguilar, Madrid, Spain)
"Poesia Argentina Actual" (1930–1960) (1961, Selection by David Martinez, Ministerio de Educacion y Justicia)
"Poesia Argentina" (1963, Selection by Instituto Don Torcuato Di Tella, Editorial del Instituto)
"40 Años de Poesia Argentina" (1920–1960) (1963, Selection by Jose Isaacson and Carlos Urquia, Ediciones Aldaba)
"Poetas Argentinos Contemporaneos" (1964, Prologue by Guillermo de Torre, Direccion de Relaciones Culturales,Ministerio de Relaciones   Exteriores y Culto)
"Seleccion Poetica Femenina" (1965, Compiled by Marta Gimenez Pastor and Jose Daniel Viacava, Direccion Nacional de Cultura)
"Antologia de la Poesia Viva Latinoamericana" (1966, Selection by Aldo Pellegrini, Seix Barral, Barcelona, Spain)
"Los Poetas del 40" (1968, Selection by Alfredo Veirave, Centro Editor de America Latina)
"Contemporary Argentine Poetry" (1969, An anthology by William Shand, Fundacion Argentina para la Poesia)

"Argentine Poetry" (1972, By Ulises Raul Pico and Ben Belitt, Bennington
     College, United States)
"Los Mejores Poemsa de la Poesia Argentina" (1974, Selection by Martini
     Real, Editorial Corregidor)
"Antologia de las Poetisas Hispanoamericanas" (1977, Selection by Catherine
     R. Perricone, Ediciones Universal, Miami, United States)
"Poesia Argentina Contemporanea" (1978, Fundacion Argentina para lPoesia)
"Open to the Sun" (1979, A Bilingual Anthology of Latin-American Women
     Poets, Edited by Nora Jacquez Wieser, Perivale Press, California,
     United States)
"Antologia de la Poesia Argentina" (1979, Selected by Raul Gustavo Aguirre
     Ediciones Fausto)
"Antologia esencial de la Poesia Argentina" (1900-1980) (1981, Selection by
     Horacio Armani, Editorial Aguilar)
"Palabra de Mujer" (1982, Selection by Jorge Boccanera, Editores Mexicanos
     Unidos, Mexico)
"Poesia Contemporanea de America Latina" (1982, Selection by Jorge
     Boccanera and Saul Ibargoyen, Editores Mexicanos Unidos, Mexico)
"Poetas de Hoy en España y America" (1982, Poesia Nueva, Madrid, Spain)
"Contemporary Women Authors of Latin America" (1983, Brooklyn College
     Press, New York, United States)
"Antologia de la Poesia Hispanoamericana" (1985, Selection by Juan Gustavo
     Cobo Borda, Fondo de Cultura Economica, Mexico)

BIBLIOGRAPHY ABOUT OLGA OROZCO

Are, Guillermo. *Suma de la poesia argentina*, Buenos Aires, Guadalupe, 1970.

Campanella, Hebe N. *La voz de la mujer en la joven poesia argentina*. En *Cuadernos Hispanoamericanos*, no 300, junio de 1975.

Cobo Borda J.G. *Poesia argentina; notas de lectura*. En *Usos de la imagi nacion*, Buenos Aires, ediciones de El Imaginero, 1984.

Colombo, Stella Maris. *Metafora y cosmovision en la poesia de Olga Orozco*. Rosario, Cuadernos Aletheia, 1983.

De Ruschi Crespo, Maria Julia. *La misma sustancia del abismo*. En *La Opinion Cultural*, 25 de enero de 1981.

Ghiano, Juan Carlos. *Poesia argentina del siglo XX*. Mexico–Buenos Aires, Fondo de Cultura Economica, 1957.

Gomez Paz, Julieta. *Dos textos sobre la poesia de Olga Orozco*. Buenos Aires, ediciones Tekne, 1980.
  –*Cuatro actitudes poeticas*. Buenos aires, Conjunta Editores, 1977.

Liscano, Juan. *Olga Orozco y su trascendente juego poetico*. Prologo a *Veintinueve poemas*, Caracas, Monte Avila, 1975.
  –*Olga Orozco y sus juegos peligrosos*. En *Descripciones*, Buenos Aires, Ediciones de la Flor–Monte Avila, 1983.

Loubet, Jorgelina. *Lo cotidiano, el fulgor y el signo*. En *Zona Franca*, no 20, setiembrioctubre, 1980.

Luzzani Bystrowicz, Telma. *Olga Orozco: poesia de la totalidad*. En Capitulo, no 112, Centro Editor de America Latina, 1981.
  –*Prologo a Olga Orozco, poesia*. Buenos Aires, Centro Editor de America Latina, 1982.

Omil, Alba. *Ensayos sobre literatura argentina*. San Miguel de Tucuman, ediciones de la Universidad, 1984.

Orphee, Elvira. *La poetica en la obra de Olga Orozco*. En America en Letras, no 2, marzo, 1984.

Pichon Riviere, Marcelo. *Multiples formas de la transparencia*. En Plural no 4, Jan, 1976.

Piña, Cristina. Prologo a *Paginas de Olga Orozco seleccionadas por la autora*, Buenos aires, Editorial Celtia, 1984.

Rebok, Maria Gabriela. *Finitud, creacion poetica y sacralidad en la obra de Olgo Orozco.* En *Revista de la sociedad Argentina de Filosofia,* no 3, Cordoba, 1985.
    -Olga Orozco y el anhelo de la unidad perdida. En *Pliego de_ poesia,* Buenos Aires, Primavera 1985.

Tacconi, Maria del Carmen. *Para una lectura simbolica de Olgo Orozco.* En Sur, no 348, Enero–junio, 1981.

Zolezzi, Emilio. *Olga Orozco o la creacion incesante.* En *Clarin,* 22 de mayo, 1975.

*H*e was born 24 June 1911 in Rojas, a small town in the Province of Buenos Aires. He completed his primary education in the Escuela No 1 of that same place.

In 1924 he was sent to La Plata, in Buenos Aires Province, where he completed secondary school and associated himself with anarchist student organizations.

In 1929 he entered the Physics & Mathematics Faculty of the La Plata National University. The next year he took part in the strikes against General Uriburu who outsted President H. Irigoyen, and joined the communist movement.

In 1934 he went to the Brussels Congress against Fascism and the War, and broke with the communist party. After a stay in Paris he went back to Argentina where he resumed his studies and married Matilde Kuminsky-Richter.

In 1938 his first son, Jorge Federico was born. Finishing his Doctorate in Physics, he was awarded a grant to work on atomic radiations at the Curie Laboratory in Paris. There he came in contact with Andre Breton and other surrealists.

In 1939 he visited the States and worked on Cosmic Rays and Relativity at the Massachusetts Institute of Technology.

In 1940 he taught in La Plata's Faculty of Physics & Mathematics and wrote his first literary collaboration for the magazine Teseo.

In 1941 he made his first contribution to the prestigious "Sur" magazine where he met other important writers, such as Borges.

In 1943 he definitevely abandoned Science and went to live for a year in a cottage in the mountains of the Province of Cordoba, where he wrote his first book "Uno y el Universo".

In 1945 his second son Mario was born, and the forementioned book was published and won the First Municipal prose Prize and the Ribbon of Honour from the Argentinian Writers' Guild (Argentores).

In 1947 due to grave financial difficulties he had to work again, and Sir Julian Huxley assigned him to UNESCO. Discontented with his situation abroad, Sabato resigned after two months. He travelled through Italy and returned to Argentina by ship. During the journey he wrote the first draft of the novel "El Tunel". Next year it was published by "Sur" after several other publishing houses had rejected it. Discovered by Albert Camus, it was translated to French, and in 1951 published by Gallimard in Paris. The same book, entitled "The Outsider" was released in English, by Borzoi Books of New York. The novel was enthusiastically praised by such writers as Thomas Mann and Graham Greene. That same year he wrote another essay "Hombres y Engranajes". In 1953 "Heterodoxia" appeared and his father Francisco Sabato died in 1955.

In 1956 he wrote "El Otro Rostro del Peronismo". In 1958 he was appointed Director of Cultural Relations of the Ministry of External Affairs, and a year later he resigned.

In 1963 his second novel "Sobre Heroes y Tumbas" appeared, and in 1964 he published two more essays: "El Escritor y sus Fantasmas" and "Tango. Discusion y Clave". Next year, his mother Juana Maria Ferrari died and the French Government awarded him the title of Chevalier des Arts et des Lettres, that had been instituted by Andre Malraux. In 1965 an album "Romance de la Muerte de Juan Lavalle" appeared in Buenos Aires. Sabato wrote the text and Eduardo Falu composed the music. Next year Editorial Losada published the first volume of his complete works.

In 1968 "Tres Aproximaciones a la Literatura de Nuestro Tiempo" appeared followed by "Itinerario" an anthology, in 1969.

In 1973 he received the Stuttgart's Prize of the Institut fur Auslands – beziehunger from Germany. Next year he published his third novel "Abbaddon El Exterminador". He was awarded the Great Honour Prize from the Argentinian Writers' Guild and also the National Recognition Prize.

In 1976 he received the Prix du Meilleur Livre Etranger in Paris for "Abbaddon El Exterminador" (L'Ange des Tenebres). The prize had been awarded to such writers as Solzhenitsyn, H. Boll, Isaac B. Singer and Garcia Marquez.

In 1979 he published "Apologias y Rechazos" and was awarded France's Chevalier de la Legion d'Honneur. That same year Spain gave him the Prize "Gran Cruz al Merito Civil".

In 1981 he published the essay "Robotizacion del Hombre". In 1983 a theatrical version of "Sobre Heroes y Tumbas" was staged in Madrid adapted by Sanchis Sinisterra. That same year he published "Paginas de Ernesto Sabato seleccionadas por el autor" an anthology of his own best material.

In 1984 he received the Gabriela Mistral Prize and the highest distinction in the Spanish Language, the Cervantes' Prize, in Madrid. Ernesto Sabato lives now with his wife Matilde in Santos Lugares, Buenos Aires, and has re-taken painting.

His works have been translated into 21 languages. He has lectured in many Universities throughout the world, among others: Paris, Columbia, Bekerley, Madrid, Warsaw, Bucharest, Bonn, Milan, Pavia, Florence.

ERNESTO SABATO

BUENOS AIRES, 1985

Santos Lugares, which in English means Holy places, is hardly 40 minutes by car from the capital. Nevertheless it feels like a typical pampean town. The railway station, principal park, church, low-level houses and the melancholic streets add up to that atmosphere – sometimes frightful – of neighbours who know one another.

It is July at six o'clock in the afternoon and is already pitch black. It is also the first time since I arrived to Argentina, that I have the feeling of the "bonaerense" (from Buenos Aires) winter. It is almost charming in comparison to the Torontonian equivalent.

Ernesto Sabato's house is not hard to find. Everybody knows where it is. Except for me, that is, since after such a long absence I had difficulties in getting there.

The owner of a drugstore near the station gives me all the necessary details adding: "you can't miss it, there are police at the entrance". His remark brings back many things. In sharp contrast with the artists and intellectuals who prefer an ivory tower, Ernesto Sabato has always practiced what he preached.

A harsh critic of both Marxism – which he fled in disillusionment – and Capitalism, and also of that new oppressive force called Technocracy, Sabato has always protected the whole man. He, whose essential and spiritual territory, is the most under attack. And particularly the Argentinian, whose aspirations of social justice and freedom have been consistently crushed over the last decades.

As president of the CONADEP (National Investigating
Comission for the Dissappeared) Ernesto Sabato is charged with
a gigantic and terrible search. It is a task which demands true
courage. And it is a task that through the years in Argentina, could
be paid with one's life.

In front of the house there are police. They ask my name
and if I'm expected. They confirm with the house and finally I step
through the house door.

Matilde, Sabato's wife, gives me a loving welcome and just
behind her comes Ernesto. The house is in semi-darkness. "I
have to have little light," says Sabato "it bothers my eyes".

It's been many years since the last time I saw him. He has
changed very little. More grey hair, the moustache a bit whiter
perhaps, but that's all.

I follow him along some corridors and we arrive in a
comfortable, austere studio. Later on Matilde will join us with
some coffee.

We start in with the immediate past and some talk of
Canada. The inevitable question comes up of why one lives there
and not in Argentina. We agree on the importance of being
married "to someone who speaks your own language". He tells
of his escape with Matilde - when she was only 16 years old -
to become his wife for life.

Sabato has always had a worried face. As if a tense and
continuous interior monologue were going on. When he speaks,
he sometimes does it with almost inhibiting authority. He puts
emphasis on certain words and there is an imperceptible air of
the country in his tone.

"You caught me feeling a bit tire, Raul" he says "we had a
very complicated lunch downtown and... I almost forgot you were
coming!"

His presence nevertheless gives off an aura of unusual
vigour. As if he were a much younger man whose physique
doesn't coincide with his long-suffering, intellectual traits.

Like Borges and Octavio Paz, he has also been awarded,
among numerous others, the Cervantes Prize. That is the
maximum Literary award in the Spanish language.

He has written "El tunel" ("The tunnel"), "Sobre heroes y tumbas" ("About heroes and tombs") and "Abaddon el exterminador" ("Abaddon the exterminator") three novels that alone win him a place among the great literary writers of the world.

If this statement seems audacious – to me it seems tardy – it's backed by writers who go from Thomas Mann and Albert Camus to Witold Grombowicz, Graham Greene and Salvatore Quasimodo.

With a Doctorate in Physics and a Grant to work in atomic radiations at the Curie Laboratory in Paris followed by Massachusetts Institute of Technology, Ernesto Sabato abandoned science and has dedicated himself to writing since 1944.

With those three works and innumerable essays – all masterpieces of lucid criticism – the writer has left a rich body of work to explain the spiritual crisis and deep fissure of the modern man. Perhaps the saying "nobody is a prophet in his own land" fits him well. I prefer the way in which Sabato says it, in one of his pages: "how could he be a genius if he lives around the corner..."

This is not the place for an essay about what Sabato has done "with" and "for" the novel. That would require someone more capable than myself and probably several books. Some of which have already been written. But let the author speak for himself, in a passage entitled "Querido y remoto muchacho" ("Dear and faraway friend") from his novel "Abaddon the exterminator".

"The novel places itself between the beginning and end of modern times. Paralleling man's rising profanation (a significant word) to this dreadful process of demythification of the world. It is for this reason that attempts to judge the novel in strictly formal terms, end in sterility. It has to be placed in this formidable total crisis of man: related to the gigantic arch that starts with Christianity. For without Christianity the uneasy conscience would have not existed. Without modern technology, desacralization, cosmic insecurity, loneliness and alienation, would have not come about.

Europe injected psychological and metaphysical unrest into their legendary tales and simple epic adventures to produce a new genre (we can now use this term) that has revealed a fantastic new terrain: the conscience of man."

* * * * *

Galvez: Ernesto do you think the place where a writer is born, where he spends his childhood, in your case Rojas, in the Province of Buenos Aires, influences his subsequent works?

Sabato: Yes, generally speaking – and in this matter in-depth psychology is right – childhood is decisive in the artistic creation. And particularly and especially in literature. In the creation of fiction.
It is true that childhood leaves very deep marks, even though they do not need to be expressed in a literary way. Fiction is a complex process – as complex as dreams – and has similar roots. Dreams don't reproduce necessarily what one has lived through while awake. It's almost always the other way round – an antagonistic act of reality. Art is also an antagonistic act of reality. You create what you don't have in most cases, and that is in response to some deeply felt need.

In fiction one therefore shouldn't expect literal descriptions. Serious fiction – which is what I believe we're talking about – is a result of strong pressure from the subconscious. And so we often find symbols and myths in it. Yes, childhood influences in an involuntary way, and weighs on the rest of one's existence. It is transubstantiated in the same mysterious way as dreams transform reality. As for myself, obviously growing up in a small Pampean village is quite different from living as a child in a highrise. We cannot conceive for example of Proust's literature arising from anything but the 6th arrondissement of Paris.

Galvez: Of course.

Sabato: Nowadays however we do have to guard against the tendency of explaining art through geographic, economic or political concepts. This was prevalent in the last century and the beginning of the twentieth. I think that art is inexplicable. It should never be explained.

Galvez: The spirit blows where it wants?

Sabato: Yes, quite so.

Galvez: Living away in Toronto, Canada, I often wonder why Argentina has produced so many artists, writers, poets and musicians - quite exceptional individuals, although as a country it doesn't function as a united social body.

Sabato: Yes, when you say "although" like that, I am reminded of Proust who said that "although" is generally an unknown "Why". In this case "although" explains why all these artists and writers have appeared in Argentina. It is not in spite of, but because of the dreadfully confused and sometimes terrible reality in which we live. I said before art is an antagonistic act. What it creates is what you don't have... The creator does not conform to the world around him. That is why he needs to create. Another reality is thereby created (not copied). How can he recreate a reality that is despicable or infamous, sad or repugnant? So in a city of non-conformists, and a society where most seem against what is happening, it is not surprising that some great artists surge to the surface.
Take a look at Czarist Russia. It can be closely compared to Argentina at the end of the last century - with its 'estancians', bureaucrats, useless generals, with its laziness and disorder. Have you read Gogol's The government Inspector? That could have happened in any small town near Buenos aires.

Galvez: That's true, you often see it in films...

Sabato: Very often. And in some of Chekov's plays too. Czarist Russia at that time had an illiteracy rate of 90%, hordes of hungry servants, an inefficient bureaucracy. Yet at the same time there were fiercely patriotic men in Russia. Speaking of writers, the patriots were Tolstoy, Dostoievski, Pushkin... practically all of them. Pushkin incited Gogol to write. Gogol would read his works to Pushkin, as in an examination. On one occasion they say Pushkin laughed so much - at Gogol's remarks - he started to cry and said "How sad Russia is". That sadness in Russia, that we see so often in Chekov, is the sadness of little towns. And that is the most fertile ground for great art.

The great artist is always a rebel. He is an outsider. And so it is not in spite of, but because of, the unforeseeable circumstances that Russia has produced one of the greatest literatures of all time. To put it another way – in a perfect society, where there are no difficulties, pain, impatience or anxiety, yes, you can have nice things such as sofas in halls and elegant decors. But you will very seldom find 'Crime and Punishment', 'The Brothers Karamatsov', or 'The Dead Souls'. So in that sense we have very little to complain about in Argentina. We have a situation that is horrendous and difficult enough...

Galvez: And in that sense stimulating.

Sabato: ...to stimulate great art. There has been, and is, great art. That's why I systematically oppose the economic classification of the term 'underdeveloped countries'. What does it mean? In the last century Russia was an underdeveloped country economically speaking. Yet it produced such greatness. Argentina was not an underdeveloped country, unless one is to apply those absurd, brutal, economic concepts to classify a culture. In our time Latin America has probably created the greatest fiction. The North Americans achieved the same heights just after the first World War. And qualifying Latin America therefore as an underdeveloped continent, by merely applying sociological and economic standards is a monstrosity. Nicaragua has produced Ruben Dario, one of the greatest poets of the Spanish language. Peru, despite its great poverty, produced Cesar Vallejo. And we are just speaking of poets. We could also mention novelists, and other creators. So going back to your original question, it is clear that it is the difficulties that encourage great art. The American example is worth remembering. It has produced one of the most important literatures in existence, while originating in a country that is obviously violent – and I'm not saying this to denigrate America, for we should appreciate a country for its great exponents, and not for its contradictions. It is the harsh existence of a pragmatic nation, fundamentally inclined to action, that has always looked askance at art. To the point where, having a so-called intellectual President (and I'm speaking of Kennedy), they killed him.

Galvez: And you think that is because they are a pragmatic nation?

Sabato: They inherited the pragmatic tradition from Britain which is also a country of action. Action and success have been their essential attributes. A man is measured by his successes.

Galvez: By what he has achieved, and not what he is.

Sabato: Yes, by what he has achieved. Take the conquest of the American West. That was a sort of epic – bloody, terrible and cruel, but undoubtedly an epic, that could only have been achieved by a very strong nation, primarily motivated by action. But obviously, that is not fertile ground for creation, nor is it a civilization that admires writers. I remember when I was in Cambridge, Mass. in 1939, none of my fellow students had heard of Faulkner. I knew him because I was a 'Barbarian'... (laughs) 'barbarian' in the noblest sense of the word means "from a nearby country". I already knew of him when I was in Paris where he had been translated, with a prologue by Sartre. But Americans hardly knew him. He had to write 'Requiem For A Nun' to gain a name of himself... And he did it on purpose. He meant to write a sensationalist novel, to become famous. That explains some-what the existence of an art form in a country like Argentina – and a continent like Latin America.

Galvez: And Argentina stands out from Latin America in that context.

Sabato: Precisely. And I would add this. Foreign teachers and journalists when they arrive here seem surprised. I don't know what they were expecting... Mexico, Peru or Ecuador perhaps. But it's not like that. Ours is a very strange country, and this accentuates the problems we were talking about. Argentina is a fractured territory between Latin America and Europe. It is not exactly Latin America – in the same way as Peru or Mexico. And it is not European in the way France and Italy are. It is a divided region. Dramatically divided.

Galvez: Yes, and it embraces both realities.

Sabato: It embraces and conflicts with both traditions, radically and culturally speaking. Now this is probably a positive factor for the production of art and particularly literature. It adds to the dramatization of the Argentinian identity, with its ambiguity, and state of spiritual conflict.
All these elements stimulate fiction.

Galvez: Do you think there is an Argentinian world view?

Sabato: Without a doubt. As there is an American point of view. We know the United States as a country – almost a handful of nations at the moment – yet despite its chaotic components, there is a coherent vision. Being one of the two most powerful nations on earth, it has disseminated its vision to all four corners.

That goes from blue jeans to jazz -jazz and all its derivatives, such as the rock music that you hear everywhere. That is the American way. Had America been a small country, the phenomenon would never have gone beyond its frontiers. There would be no need for explanations about why Japanese and Russian kids wear blue jeans. Its extraordinary power - physical, economic, material and political explains all this. Yes, there is an American way of seeing the world, as there is an Argentinian, with its own peculiar characteristics, though, as we are not super powers, matters don't have such grave repercussions. You can tell an Argentinian when you are abroad. I, for example, have been in Paris and seen one walking towards me. And I have crossed to the other side of the street. Why? Because I suspect he is going to start talking about Buenos Aires - the difficulties, the bitterness. So I say to myself, "that is Argentinian, let's go somewhere else!" There is a certain way of dressing and even walking - there's a certain something about them.

Galvez: There's a certain skin tone too, it seems to me.

Sabato: Yes, and there is also something here that unifies the son or grandson of Italians, the grandson of Basques, the grandson of Jews and the grandson of Arabs... it's very typical. And that indicates a strong spiritual force. Contrary to popular argentinian belief it is a sign of strong character. Take a look at the language which reveals the innermost spirit of a nation. It is the only Spanish-speaking country to have resisted banishing the familiar term 'vos' (you) from the language, despite the recommendation of the Royal Spanish Academy.
Today the best Argentinian writers use it. Our language differs from that of Madrid - not only in its accent, but also in its syntax and vocabulary. Then there's the tango, - which so typifies our character. Very strange. So many theses have been put forward on the dance...
I myself wrote an essay on the metaphysics of the tango. The music is introverted - as Discepolo said "it is a sad thought you dance to". You don't have that in Brazilian music - it's happy. Caribbean music is fabulously euphoric. But the Argentinian tango with its songs from Buenos Aires is dramatic, introverted and sad. That reveals something about the Argentinian...

Galvez: Melancholy.

Sabato: It is melancholic. The fusion of two important elements - two solitudes or lonelinesses if you like. When immigration began on a large scale, the 'paisanos' (what in any other country are called 'gauchos'), emmigrated from the desert to the big city in search of work. Settling in the suburbs, after they were hired in the factories of Buenos Aires or Rosario, they encountered other lonely people – the European immigrants. And both missed having women folk. The tango brought together the two lonelinesses in the suburban whore-houses. That's where the tango was born. The same as for jazz in the States. The whore-house was the club where lonely men met. The 'paisano's' music was the 'milonga', which epitomizes solitude. Some European songs are melancholic – take the Portuguese 'fado'. Then there's the Napolitan 'canzonette' which is sad too. Fused with the 'paisano's' music, it accounts for the drama of the dance and its music.

Galvez: Some historians say that Argentina has been in crisis since the '30s, while others maintain that it has been like that for much longer. But this cannot be entirely blamed on the Argentinian ruling class. The States and England must shoulder some of the blame. The States for example didn't like the idea of a United States of the south...

Sabato: Yes. You know that at the turn of the century, we seemed to have one of the brightest futures in the world. Many historians and foreign observers felt that Argentina would become the United States of the south. It was the fifth most wealthy country in the world with excellent level of nutrition and literacy. We had a very high standard of living. Then it began to fall. It is said that certain groups were interested in stopping the developments and were keen to maintain the state of dependency from which we now suffer. That could be so... I don't know, but then all things are possible from the 'great capitals of the world'. For a long time England was interested in keeping Argentina subjugated. There is a well-known saying: "England, the metropolis/the industry/the factory: Argentina, the farm/the rich reserve of raw materials". The English had vested interests in maintaining that dependency, that link between producer-farmer and factory. I remember when I was a little boy, everything came from England: the toilets, bathtubs, sinks, china, knives, forks. Even the gin came from England! (laughs). And they wanted to keep that fantastic market – a market that provided them with meat and wheat, but above all meat. So, instead of using our strength and initiative to fight these colossal forces, we became dependent. It's hard to imagine how strong the British Empire was at the beginning of the century. It's over now.

Galvez: Yes, it has almost returned to its own island.

Sabato: But what a great empire they had in the Indian era!
It was at that time that an English Lord in parliament described
Argentina as "the pearl of the British crown..." England and
France were the two great tutors in the everyday life as well as
culturally-speaking.

Galvez: In addition, Murena (Argentine writer) wrote that
Argentina, curiously enough, never looked towards Spain as a
cultural model, but rather to France and England.

Sabato: People used to dress in the English manner.
Anybody with any kind of money wore English cashmere. There
was no choice. And we children wore English-tailored suits. If
possible parents sent their children to Oxford or Cambridge for
their higher education.

Galvez: On another topic Ernesto, and going back to the
subject of your achievements -- you received the Cervantes Prize
for Literature. What does that mean to an Argentine or a Spanish
writer?

Sabato: It was instituted about 5-6 years ago. Latin
Americans such as Borges, Octavio Paz and now me have won
it. It is a very important prize, and considered to probably be the
most important in the language... I feel honoured and even stimulated at having received it.
I think it's the highest a Spanish writer can aspire to.

Galvez: Do you think that literature can improve language?
I ask you, because after 6 years away from Argentina, I sensed
a corruption in the language you hear in the streets. The people
in Buenos Aires express themselves badly. Perhaps it's a different story in the rest of the country.

Sabato: The modern world is mediocre. A Spanish friend
told me the other day that the same thing has happened in Spain.
No one speaks properly anymore. Language is becoming impoverished, due to journalism, television, and advertising. I said
jokingly to a friend the other day that television is the opium of
the people, to paraphrase the idea that religion is the opium of the
people.
Television is a gigantic calamity. So is bad journalism. They
impoverish the language, and transform it into a bundle of cliches
and stereotypes. That is obviously very sad while it is a universal

phenomenon. But fundamentally one should judge a nation's
culture by its great writers, not by the language spoken in the bars
and the soccer stadium. Language has to be judged by its highest
exponents. And it seems that throughout Latin America, as well
as in Spain, the language of Cervantes has not decayed. What is
more it has produced some formidable literature. Now, of course,
one looks at populist TV, and one feels indignant. But I've seen
this in many places. Yes. Now, for example, no one can distin-
guish between the terms to listen and to hear any more. That's
not only in Buenos Aires. TV series dubbed by the Puerto Ricans
and Mexicans fail to make the difference too. One day a woman
journalist who had been trying to see me for an interview for
some time, finally reached me by telephone.
We were trying to set-up a mutually convenient time, when
suddenly she said "I don't *escucho'* (*listen*) very well. I replied
"Miss, you are insolent. If you don't *listen* well, after begging for
this interview, you are insolent and rude.
You probably meant that you couldn't *hear* me well, because you
must have been *listening* very attentively". I mean, a journalist
who mixes up *listening* and *hearing*... This happens all too often,
and not only in Argentina. It is due to the sub-culture that stan-
dardization brings, in which journalism, radio, television and all
such instruments impoverish and dehumanize man.

Galvez: Yes, it is a phenomenon that goes beyond frontiers.

Sabato: I don't know the English language well enough, but
I sense the same may have happened in the United States.

Galvez: Yes it has, and also in Canada.

Sabato: So we see it as a universal phenomenon. And that
is not speaking of the grotesque extremes one hears in the
Hispanic communites of the States. They mix up Spanish and
English in the same word - take for example 'marketa' which
means 'market'!

Galvez: Yes, and new words are invented. But isn't that
valid? Isn't it sometimes a way of keeping language alive?

Sabato: I've written several essays on the subject - that
perhaps you've read. They are against the academics and in
defense of living language. But living language is not made by the
people, that is to say 'the people' in the narrowest sense.
For language is made up of two extremes - the general population
and then the great writers. In the middle you have the Academy,

which, in my opinion, is of no use.
That's why I have never joined the Academy, for it would be like
betraying something for which I have always fought. Language
is alive/life. Every language is life/alive. Every language transforms itself. As Humboldt (the first linguistic theorist to present
the problem) observed, language is not static but rather in motion.
Energy in motion. In this sense, we have to accept the transfor-
mations that reality brings us. But I think that today things differ
from the era in which the Romance languages evolved from Latin.
Nowadays mass communication has hugely influenced yet impoverished the language. This is a new development in the
history of humanity. Totally new...

Galvez: Accelerated perhaps by the mass media.

Sabato: ...by the power and transcendency of the mass
media. This is a terrible phenomenon, manipulated as it is by the
mass media in most countries, and against which I don't know
what can be done.

Galvez: I would like to touch on a delicate matter now. As
the Head of the CONADEP (National Committee for the Investigation of the 'desaparecidos'), what do you think about the legal
proceedings against the military now under way in Buenos Aires?

Sabato: I think this is an exemplary trial, executed with all
the dignity, seriousness and solemnity required to a trial of such
importance.
There are now the maximum guarantees that a civilized country
can offer. In a civilized society, crime should be punished. In this
case there were abominable crimes. This doesn't mean that all
the Armed Forces were guilty – not at all. Neither the court, nor
the people think that. It is a question of discriminating – the ones
who have committed crimes are in the minority.
The vast majority are not delinquents. We therefore hope and
desire that that small minority is punished.

Galvez: A final question. Six years in Toronto have shown
me that Canadians are searching, deeply searching for their own
identity and what it means to be Canadian. What would you say
to its young artists and writers?

Sabato: I noticed that search when talking to some Canadians. It's a moving anxiety – really, very moving. It would be
more serious if they were not serious. The very fact they are
worried means they are on the way to solving it. Canada is a

country that has been a supplier of raw materials to a foreign power. Now I believe that we're going to find out what the Canadian way of seeing things is. And the new generation, in literature, art and in film is going to find its own way. It's not an easy thing, for it is subtle and will only reveal itself through many artistic works. We shouldn't wait for miracles in one work alone. Argentinians understand the problem for we've had our own struggles. The difference is that we were a colony in the 19th century, and for 150 years now we've been searching for our identity.

Canada's experience is unfinished. It's still, in a way, an append-age to the two empires -- Great Britain and the United States. Some Canadians I spoke to amazed me with their intensity and anxiety. Of course they don't need to be a majority. A minority is quite enough, but it has to be a thinking minority, a doer minority that will produce great works and discover the actions that identify the Canadian people.

PRINCIPAL WORKS BY ERNESTO SABATO

(Original title, year of first edition and publishing house. Unless otherwise noted, all originated in Buenos Aires, Argentina).

"Uno y el Universo" (1945, Sudamericana)
"El Tunel" (1948, Sur)
"Hombres y Engranajes" (1951, Emece)
"Heterodoxia" (1953, Emece)
"El Otro Rostro del Peronismo" (1956, Imprenta Lopez)
"El caso Sabato; torturas y libertad de prensa; carta abierta al Gral.
    Aramburu" (1956, Privately Published, Buenos Aires)
"Sobre Heroes y Tumbas" (1961, Compania General Fabril Editora)
"El Escritor y sus Fantasmas" (1963, Aguilar)
"Tango. Discusion y Clave" (1963, Losada)
"Obras de Ficcion" (1966, Losada)

"Pedro Henriquez Ureña" (1967, Ediciones Culturales Argentinas)
"Tres Aproximaciones a la Literatura de Nuestro Tiempo" (1968, Editorial
    Universitaria, Santiago de Chile)
"Itinerario" (1969, Sur)
"La convulsion politica y social de nuestro tiempo" (1969, Edicom)
"Abbadon el Exterminador" (1974, Sudamericana)
"Apologias y Rechazos" (1979, Seix Barral, Barcelona, Spain)
"Robotizacion del Hombre" (1981, Centro Editor de America Latina)
"Paginas de Ernesto Sabato seleccionadas por el Autor" (1983, Editorial
Celtia, Coleccion Escritores Argentinos de Hoy)

BIBLIOGRAPHY ABOUT SABATO

Articles:

The following bibliography of Sabato's miscellaneous journalistic writings, while not exhaustive, is representative of those articles most characteristic of him as an essayist. A few other articles of interest because of their historical importance in his career are also included.

"Algunas reflexiones sobre el *nouveau roman*," *Sur*, No. 285 (Novermber–December 1963), pp. 42–67.

"Aquella patria de nuestra infancia," *Sur*, No. 237 (November–December 1955), pp. 102–106.

"Arte y literatura: Realidad y ficcion," *El Litoral* (Buenos Aires), January 28, 1962.

"Arthur Stanley Eddington," Sur, No. 123 (January 1945), pp. 38–48.

"Borges y Borges el argentino y la metafisica," *Vida Universitaria*, XIV, No. 681 (April 12, 1964), 3–18.

"Contra la paralisis," *Sur*, No. 119 (September 1944), pp. 118–19.

"Cortes Pla: Galileo Galilei," *Sur*, No. 103 (April 1943), pp. 98–101.

"Desagravio a Borges," *Sur*, No. 94 (July 1942), pp. 30–31.

"El caso 'Lolita,'" *Sur*, No. 260 (September–October 1959), p. 57.

"En torno de Borges," *Casa de las Americas*, III No. 17–18 (1963) pp. 7–12.

"George Gamow: *Mr. Tompkins in Wonderland*," *Sur*, No. 97 (October 1942), pp.117–19.

"George Russell Harrison: *Atomos en accion*," *Sur*, No. 93 (June 1942), pp.62–67.

"Julio Rey Pastor, *La ciencia y la tecnica en el descubrimiento de America*," *Revista de Filologia Hispanica*, IV (1942), pp. 369–99.

"La deidad," *Sur*, No. 268 (January–February 1961), pp. 79–91.

"La fuente muda," *Sur*, No. 157 (November 1947), pp. 24–65.

"La unica paz admisible," *Sur* No. 129 (July 1945),pp.28–43.

"Los relatos de Jorge Luis Borges," *Sur*, No. 125 (March 1945), pp. 69–75.

"Luca Pacioli: *La Divina Proporcion*," *Sur*, No. 142 (August 1946), pp.90–99.

"Manuel Galvez: *Vida de Sarmiento*; Renee Pereyra Olazabal: *Mitre*," *Sur*, No. 129 (July 1945), pp. 114–16.

"Max Planck: *Adonde va la ciencia*" *Sur*, No. 84 (September 1941), pp. 67–70.

"On Alfven's Hypothesis of a 'Cosmic Cyclotron,'" *Physical Review*, Vol. 55, No. 12 (June 15, 1939), pp. 1272–1273.

"Palabras, palabras, palabras," *Sur*, No. 267 (November–December 1960)< pp. 38–41.

"Realidad y realismo en la literatura de nuestro tiempo," *Comentario*, No. 33. (1962), pp. 10–21.

"Significado de Pedro Henriquez Ureña," *La Gaceta* (Tucuman, Argentina), September 5, 1965.

"Sobre el derrumbe de nuestro tiempo," *Sur*, No. 192–194 (October–November–December 1950)m pp. 86–92.

"Sobre el sentido comun," *Sur*, No. 121 (November 1944), pp. 64–65.

"Sobre *Heterodoxia*," *Sur*, No. 228 (May–June 1954), p. 128.

"Sobre la metafisica del sexo," *Sur*, No. 209–210 (March–April 1952), pp. 24–47; and no.213–214 (July–August 1952),pp. 158–61.

"Sobre 'Norteamerica la hermosa,'" *Sur*, No 195–96 (January–February 1951), pp. 67–69.

Selected Bibliography

"Tango, cancion de Buenos Aires," *Negro sobre Blanco*, No. 29 (1963), pp. 19–22

"Ucar, Maya y Otero: *El gran parto*," *Sur*, No. 198 (April 1951), pp. 72–73.

Translations:

The following translations are of *El tunel:*

The Outsider. New York: Knopf, 1950.

Tunneln. Stockholm: Skoglunds Bokforlag, 1951.

Le Tunnel. Paris: Gallimard, 1956.

Der Maler und das Fenster. Vienna: Rohrer, 1958.

O tunel. Rio de Janeiro: Editora civilizacao Brasileira, 1961.

Tunel. Warsaw: PIW, 1963.

TunelLul. Bucharest: Editura P.L.U., 1965.
> An Italian edition by Feltrinelli (Milan) is forthcoming, and fragments have appeared in the Japanese newspaper, Akoku Nippo. Four translations of Sobre heroes y tumbas have been published:

Sopra erpo e tpmbe. Milan: Feltrinelli, 1965.

Bohaterach i Grobach. Warsaw: PIW, 1966.

Alejandra. Paris: Editions du Seuil, 1967.
> *Uber Helden und Graber.* Wiesbaden: Limes Verlag, 1967.
> An English translation by Holt, Rinehart and Winston is soon to appear

Recordings:

Retirada y Muerte de Lavalle. Buenos Aires: Philips, 1965.
> Sabato reads excerpts from the Lavalle episode of *Sobre Heroes y tumbas*; musical accompaiment is by Eduardo Falu, Mercedes Sosa, and the chorus of Francisco Javier Ocampo.

Ernesto Sabato por el mismo. Autobiografia. Buenos Aires: AMB
> Discografica, 1967. Fragments of *Sobre heroes y tumbas, Hombres y engranajes, Uno y el universo,* and *El tunel* as read by Sabato.

SECONDARY SOURCES

BIBLIOGRAPHY ABOUT

Avellaneda, Andres. "Novela e ideologia en 'Sobre heroes y tumbas' de Ernesto Sabato." *Nuevos Aires*, No. 7 (1972). 55–71.

Azancot, Leopoldo. "*El escritor y sus fantasmas,*" *Indice de Artes y Letras*, XVII, No. 186 (July 1964), 31. A review of Sabato's ideas concerning literature, the role of art, and the writings of Jorge Luis Borges.

Bacarisse, S. *Contemporary Latin American Fiction*. Edinburgh, Scottish Academic Press, 1980.

Beuchat, Cecilia. "Psicoanalisis y Argentina en una novela de Ernesto Sabato." *Taller de letras*, No. 1 (1971), 38–43.

Bruno, Ricardo. "Ernesto Sabato habla fuerte y claro." *Leoplan* (1964). An interview in which Sabato discusses his novels, current literature, and some of his future plans.

Brushwood, J.S. "Ernesto Sabato: *Hombres y engranajes,*" *Books Abroad*, Vol. 26, No. 3 (Summer 1952), 281–82. An analysis of one of   Sabato's most important essays in which the reviewer relates Sabato's inter‘ pretation of life to that of Nicholas Berdyaev and Jean Paul Sartre.

Buonocore, Domingo. "*El escritor y sus fantasmas,* por Ernesto Sabato," *Universidad*, No. 58 (1964), 416–17. Summarizes Sabato's latest collection of essays with a general evaluation of him as an essayist more than as a novelist.

Canal Feijoo, Bernardo. "En torno a una 'nouvelle' de Ernesto Sabato," *Escritura*, III No. 7 (1949), 98–101. Analyzes *El tunel* with special consideration of the enigmatic personality of Juan Pablo Castel.
----------. "Ernesto Sabato: *Sobre heroes y tumbas,*" *Sur*, No. 276 (May-June 1962), 90–99. An extensive analysis and interpretation of the second novel and especially valuable for its consideration of the role of abnormal psychology in the work.

Castellanos, Carmelina de. "Dos personajes de una novela argentina." *Cuadernos hispanoamericanos*, No. 232 (1969), 149–60.

Castillo, Abelardo. "*Sobre heroes y tumbas,*" *Indice de Artes ky Letras* XVI, No. 167 (December 1962), 31–32. Important analytical review of Sabato's second novel in which the author compares it with other works of contemporary literature.

Catania, Carlos. *Sabato, entre la idea y la sangre*. Costa Rica, Editorial Costa Rica, Universidad, 1973.

Cebollero, C.Q. *Entrando en El tunel de Ernesto Sabato*. Puerto Rico. Uprex, 1971.

Cersosimo, Emilse Beatriz. *"Sobre heroes y tumbas"*: *de los caracteres a la metafisica*. Buenos Aires: Editorial Sudamericana, 1972.

Coddou, Marcelo. "La teoria del ser nacional argentino en *Sobre heroes y tumbas*." Atenea, 45 (1968), 57–71.

Cordero, Nestor Luis. "A la busqueda de la realidad," *Entrega* (May 1962), 8. A review of *Sobre heroes y tumbas* in which the critic finds a fundamental weakness in the delineation of the novel's heroes.

Correa, Maria Angelica. *Genio y figura de Ernesto Sabato*. Buenos Aires: Editorial Universitaria de Buenos Aires, 1972.

Cortes, Nelly. "El escritor 'inconforme' Ernesto Sabato," *Indice de Artes y Letras*, XVI, nO. 158 (mARCH 1962), 19–20. Biography and general survey of Sabato's writings followed by an interview in which he answers questions concerning his essays and novels.

Dellepiane, Angela B. "Del barroco y las modernas tecnicas en Ernesto Sabato," *Revista Iberoamericana de Bibliografia*, XV, No. 3 (July–September 1965), 226–50. An analysis of *Sobre heroes y tumbas* from the point of view of the multiplicity of its themes and a comparison of it with *El tunel*.

——————. *Ernesto Sabato, El Hombre y su obra*. New York: Las Americas Publishing Company, 1969. One of the most complete studies of Sabato and his literary works. Contains a valuable bibliography.

"Dialogo con Ernesto Sabato," *El Escarabajo de Oro*, No. 5 (February 1962), 4–6, 20. Sabato discusses his writings and gives his thoughts on contemporary literature in general.

Eandi, Hector. "Carta a Ernesto Sabato," *Comentario*, X, No. 36 (1963), 71–74, 79. In a letter ostensibly directed to Sabato the author analyzes the themes and the four major protagonists of *Sobre heroes y tumbas*.

"Ensayo sobre la cancion porteña," *La Nacion* (Buenos Aires), August 8, 1964. A summary of Sabato's essays which includes many of the disparate ideas on the "Song of Buenos Aires" found within the volume.

Eyzaguirre, Luis B. "'Rayuela', 'Sobre heroes y tumbas', 'El astillero': busqueda de la identidad individual en la novela hispanoamericana contemporanea." *Nueva narrativa hispanoamericana*, 2, 2 (1972), 101–18.

Fernandez Suarez, Alvaro. "Ernesto Sabato: *Heterodoxia*," Sur, No. 224
　　　(September–October 1953), 129–32. A rather unfavorable review of
　　　Sabato's second volume of essays which at the same time praises
　　　his ability to present and sustain philosophic ideas.

––––––––––. "Ernesto Sabato: *Hombres y Engranajes*," Sur, No. 204
　　　(Octber 1951), pp. 71–74. analyzes the essay in terms of it concern
　　　for man and his feelings of desperation and isolation in a rational
　　　world; the critic concludes with the opinion that Sabato's
　　　solution to the problem presented is obscure.

Flores, Angel. "Magical Realism in Spanish American Fiction." *Hispania*
　　　XXXVIII, No. 2 (May 1955), 187–92. Discusses the technique of
　　　magical Realism in Western literature and treats *El tunel* as a
　　　representative work of this movement.

Georgescu, P.A. *Literatura hispano–americana*. Craiova (Rumania), Scrisul
　　　Romanesc, 1979.

Giacoman, Helmy y otros. *Homenaje a Ernesto Sabato*. New York, Anaya–Las
　　　Americas, 1973. (Hay otra edicion publicada por Grupo Editorial de
　　　Madrid.)

–––––––– *Los personajes de Ernesto Sabato*. Buenos Aires, Emece Editores,
　　　1972.

Gibbs, Beverly J. "'El tunel': Portrayal of Isolation," *Hispania*, XLVIII,
　　　No. 3 (September 1965), 429–36. An analytical study of *El tunel* as
　　　a portrayal of Juan Pablo Castel's existential isolation.

––––––––––. "Spacial treatment in the Contemporary Psychological Novel of
　　　Argentina," *Hispania*, XLV, No. 3 (September 1962), 410–14. A
　　　discussion of the novels of Bianco, Mallea, Sabato, Canto, and
　　　Mazzanti which develops the theory that spaciality forms a
　　　background against which the personalities of the protagonists are
　　　delineated; Castel and *El tunel* are analyzed from this point of
　　　view.

Gonzalez, Abelardo. "*El tunel*," Sur, No. 211–12 (May–June 1952), 163–65.
　　　Evaluates the film version of *El tunel* in which Sabato colaborated
　　　with the director, Leon Klimovsky, to produce a motion picture of
　　　outstanding merit, especially in regard to its interpretation of the role
　　　of Buenos Aires in the original story.

Gudino Kramer, L. "*Sobre heroes y tumbas*, por Ernesto Sabato," Universi
　　　dad, No. 58 (1963), 406–408. A good analysis of the second novel
　　　from the standpoint of the four plot divisions and of the symbolism
　　　of the several protagonists.

Harris, Yvonne J. "Ernesto Sabato: *El tunel*," *Books Abroad*, Vol. 26, No. 2 (Spring 1952), 185. An excellent short review of *El tunel*, which points out the novel's emphasis on the tortured and incoherent workings of Castel's neurotic mind.

Hayes, Alfred. "A Misunderstood Criminal," New York *Herald Tribune*, May 14, 1950. A general analysis of Sabato's first novel based on the English translation published in 1950.

Holzapfel, Tamara. "El 'Informe sobre ciegos' o el optimismo de la voluntad." *Revista Iberoamericana*, 38 (1972), 95–103.

——————. "Metaphysical Revolt in Ernesto Sabato's *Sobre heroes y tumbas*." *Hispania*, 52 (1969), 857–63.

——————. "*Sobre heroes y tumbas*, novela del siglo." *Revista Iberoamericana*, 34 (1968), 117–21.

Hornos Paz, Octavio A. El escritor frente a si mismo," *La Nacion*, March 29, 1964, 4. A critical analysis of the three textual divisions of *El escritor y sus fantasmas.*

Jimenez-Grullon, I. *Anti-Sabato o E. Sabato: un escritor dominado por fantasmas.* Maracaibo (Venezuela), Universidad del Zulia, 1968.

Jones, Willis K. "Ernesto Sabato: *Uno y el universo*," *Books Abroad*, Vol. 20, No. 3 (Summer 1946), 321. General analysis of the first volume of essays in which the reviewer concludes that the eighty essays all contain a great deal of common sense.

"Lavalle: una leyenda de Sabato en guitarra criolla," *Confirmado*, May 7, 1965, 45. Sabato's recording is reviewed with a historical and critical analysis of the role of Juan Lavalle in *Sobre heroes y tumbas.*

"Llega Ernesto Sabato," *Indice de Artes y Letras*, XVI, No. 167 (December 1962), 32. Describes Sabato's arrival at Barajas Airport in Madrid and evaluates the writer's personality.

Liberman, Arnoldo. "Carta de Buenos Aires," *Revista de la Universidad de Mexico*, Vol. XVL4I, No. 5 (January 1962), 20–21. Views Sabato as an active protagonist in the tumultuous events of the twentieth century instead of a detached intellectual.

Lichtblau, Myron. "Forma y estructura en algunas novelas argentinas contemporaneas," *Humanitas*, No. 4 (1963), 285–98. As a part of his study of various contemporary Argentine novels the author makes an analysis of *El tunel* pointing out its picaresque and *tremendista* tendencies.

Lipp, Solomon. "Ernesto Sabato: Sintoma de una epoca," *Journal of Inter-American Studies*, Vol. VIII, No. 1 (January 1966), 142–55. Probably the best overview of Sabato's essays and novels. Considers all of his writings except for the volumes of essays published after *Sobre heroes y tumbas.*

Lombardi, L.B. de. *Aproximaciones criticas a la narrativa de Ernesto Sabato.* Maracaibo (Venezuela), Universidad del Zulia, 1978.

Lorenz, Gunter W. "Ernesto Sabato..." In his *Dialog mit Lateinamerika...* (Tubingen: Horst Erdmann, 1970). pp. 39–131.

Ludmer, Iris Josefina. "Ernesto Sabato y un testimonio del fracaso." *Boletin de literaturas hispanicas,* 5 (1963), 83–100.

Martinez, N. *Ernesto Sabato.* Buenos Aires, Libreria del Colegio, 1974.

Martinez, Z. Nelly. "Fernando Vidal Olmos y el surrealismo: una conversacion con Ernesto Sabato." *Sin nombre,* 2, 3 (1972), 60–64.
––––––––––. "El 'Informe sobre ciegos' y Fernando Olmos, poeta vidente." *Revista iberoamericana,* 38 (1972), 627–39.

Maturo, Graciela. *Ernesto Sabato.* Buenos Aires, Centro Editor de America Latina, 1981.

Murtagh, Maria Isabel. *Paginas vivas de Ernesto Sabato.* Buenos Aires, Kapelusz, 1974.

Neyra, Joaquin. *Ernesto Sabato.* Buenos Aires, Serie Argentinos en las Letras, Ministerio de cultura y Educacion, 1973.

Oberhelman, H.D. *Ernesto Sabato.* New York, Twayne's World Authors Series, 1970.

Olguin, Manuel. "Ernesto Sabato: *Uno y el universo,*" *Books Abroad,* Vol. 21, No. 2 (Spring 1947), 201–202. A review of the first volume of essays which the reviewer finds unusual because of its use of science as a springboard to philosophy.

Ortega Peña, Rodolfo. "Letras argentinas," *Ficcion,* No. 83 (July–august 1962), 55–57. An analysis of Sabato as a novelist with special consideration of the use of vagueness and suggestivity in the second novel.

Pacuraru, F. *Porfiluri hispano–americane contemporane,* Bucarest, 1968.

Perez, G.R. *Historia y critica de la novela hispanoamericana.* Bogota, Circulo de Lectores, 1978.

Petersen, John Fred. "Ernesto Sabato: Essayist and Novelist," dissertation, University of Washington, 1963. Available from University Microfilms, Inc., Ann Arbor, Michigan. One of the most comprehensive and com plete studies of Sabato's works up to the year 1961.

——————. "Sabato's 'El Tunel': More Freud than Sartre," *Hispania*, L, No. 2 (May 1967), 271–76. Attempts to relate the content of *El tunel* to a universally valid fact of human psychology: the Oedipus complex.

Polakovic, E, *La clave para la obra de E. Sabato*. Buenos Aires, Ediciones Universidad del Salvador, 1981.

Pollmann, L. *La Nueva Novela en Francia y en Iberoamerica*. Madrid, Gredos, 1971.

Rodriguez Monegal, Emir. "Por una novela novelesca y metafisica." *Mundo nuevo*, No. 5 (1966), 5–21.

Roggiano, Alfredo A. "Ernesto Sabato" in *Diccionario de la literatura latinoamericana*. Washington: Pan American Union, 1961. An excellent biography of Sabato and a consideration of his writings up to the second novel. Contains a bibliography of other critical studies.

Sanchez Riva, Arturo. "Ernesto Sabato: *El tunel*," Sur, No. 169 (November 1948), 82–87. Castel's personality as the central idea of *El tunel* is the subject of this critical analysis.

——————. "Ernesto Sabato: Uno y el universo," Sur, No. 135 (January 1946), 101–106. In this analysis of Sabato's first collection of essays the critic views the work as an attempt by man to find truth and his place in life.

Souza, Raymond D. "Fernando as Hero in Sabato's 'Sobre heroes y tumbas'." *Hispania*, 55 (1972), 241–46.

Umana Portillo, H.E. *Sabato y el Universo*. Guatemala, Ediciones de la

Universidad de San Carlos de Guatemala, 1976.

Wainerman, L. *Sabato y el misterio de los ciegos*. Buenos aires, Editorial Losada, 1971. (Hay otra edicion de Castaneda, 1978.)

Novelistas hispanoamericanos de hoy. Madrid, Taurus, 1976.

Mitos y personajes literarios. Buenos Aires, Castaneda, 1980.

Petersen, John Fred. "Ernesto Sabato: Essayist and Novelist." Dissertation, University of Washington, 1963. Available from University Microfilms, Inc., Ann Arbor, Michigan. One of the most comprehensive and complete studies of Sabato's works up to the year 1961.

———. "Sabato's 'El Túnel': More Freud than Sartre." Hispania 1, No. 2 (May 1967), 271-76. Attempts to relate the content of El Túnel and to a universally valid fact of human psychology; the Oedipus complex.

Wainerman, L. La clave para la obra de E. Sabato. Buenos Aires, Universidad del Salvador, 1941.

Dellepiane, A. La Nueva Novela, in France y en Paris America, Mexico, Siglo

Rodriguez Monegal, Emir. "Un test severo: la crisis y la metafisica." Mundo nuevo, No. 5 (1966),

Bastianini, Alberto A. "Ernesto Sabato." la Devoción de la literatura hispanoamericana. Washington, Pan American Union, 1961. An excellent biography of Sabato and a comparison of his earlier two novels. Contains a bibliography of other criticism.

Dendle, Brian. Ernesto Sabato. Sur, No. 169 (November 1956), 82-85. Dendle's commentary on the central idea of El Túnel as the subject of this critical analysis.

———. "Ernesto Sabato: Hoy y el universo." Sur, No. 138 (January 1944), 101-106. In this analysis of Sabato's first collection of essays, the critic views the work as an attempt by man to find truth and his place in life.

Souza, Raymond D. "Fernando as Hero in Sabato's Sobre héroes y tumbas." Hispania 55 (1972), 241-46.

Lannoy, Paul. El to. Sabato y el Universo Existencialista. Buenos Aires, Centro Editor de América Latina, 1974.

Wainerman, L. Sabato y el misterio de los ciegos. Buenos Aires, Editorial Losada, 1971. (Biblioteca estudios de Castellanos, 1978.)

Yelin, Julio. Ernesto Sabato. Madrid, Marcha, 1967.